Learn Japanese In 4 Weeks Or Less!

A Practical Guide To Make Japanese Look Easy! EVEN For Beginners

Table Of Contents

Introduction

In this book you will find highly informative lessons that will help language learners achieve proficiency in the Japanese language in one month or less.

Many English speakers find Japanese a difficult language to learn because it is vastly different from their mother tongue. The Japanese language uses three sets of scripts for writing and phonetics. Its grammar, vocabulary, and intonation are unique. Except for the use of Chinese Kanji in its writing system, Japanese isn't quite similar to other languages.

Japanese is not that difficult to learn. It has fewer tenses, does not require subject-verb agreement, and has relatively inflexible word order. This book provides all the important strategies and techniques you will need to overcome the language barrier and typical challenges of learning the Japanese language.

It was designed to provide a reliable resource material for learning the essentials of the Japanese language quickly and easily. It features grammar lessons, vocabulary listing, useful phrases, and other important language skills such as counting, telling time and date, and using color names. It uses a straightforward yet comprehensive approach to impart fundamental language concepts in a more interesting and fun way.

Let's begin the journey.

Chapter 1: Japanese Writing System and Phonetics

Nihongo, or the Japanese language, is spoken by approximately 130 million people around the world. It is the national language of Japan, or Nihon in Japanese.

Japanese uses two native scripts: Hiragana, and Katakana. These scripts are referred to as kana and they are basically different versions of the same sounds. The Japanese alphabet does not consist of letters but character sets. Hiragana is the primary character set in Japanese. Katakana is primarily used for foreign words.

Japanese also uses Chinese characters, called Kanji, extensively in its writing system. Kanji accounts for approximately 2,000 characters or 95% of Japanese written text. The Japanese language uses more than 40,000 Kanji. In lieu of spaces between characters, Kanji is used to mark the separation of words in a sentence. It is also used to distinguish between homophones.

To learn Japanese efficiently, you have to learn the three scripts in this order: Hiragana, Katakana, and Kanji.

In the following sections, you will learn that every Hiragana and Katakana character corresponds to a vowel or consonant + vowel sound combination with the exception of two characters, namely, ん」 and 「ン」. While this system is straightforward, Japanese pronunciation is not exactly simple. The fixed syllable sound structure can, in fact, make learning proper intonation in Japanese a challenge.

Hiragana

Hiragana is primarily used for writing native Japanese words. It is the basic phonetic script in Japanese. A hiragana represents one syllable. Contemporary Japanese writing uses 46 hiragana and an additional set of 25 diacritics.

Hiragana is a simplified version of Kanji, a more complex script set which is used for different purposes. It can be used in place of kanji characters. Some Hiragana characters are used to accompany verbs and some are used as particles. Additionally, there are native Japanese words that have no equivalent in kanji and must be written in Hiragana.

Japanese have five vowels: the "aiueo". Except for "n", all Hiragana characters end with a vowel. All Japanese "consonants" are pronounced in the same way as their English counterpart except for "r". The Japanese "r" is rolled and sounds somewhere between the consonants "d", "l", and "r".

Here are the 46 basic Hiragana characters:

	A	I	U	E	O
	あ (a)	い (i)	う (u)	え (e)	お (o)
K	か (ka)	き (ki)	く (ku)	け (ke)	こ (ko)
S	さ (sa)	し (shi)	す (su)	せ (se)	そ (so)
T	た (ta)	ち (chi)	つ (tsu)	て (te)	と (to)
N	な (na)	に (ni)	ぬ (nu)	ね (ne)	の (no)
H	は (ha)	ひ (hi)	ふ (fu)	へ (he)	ほ (ho)
M	ま (ma)	み (mi)	む (mu)	め (me)	も (mo)
Y	や (ya)		ゆ (yu)		よ (yo)
R	ら (ra)	り (ri)	る (ru)	れ (re)	ろ (ro)
W	わ (wa)				を (wo/o)
N	ん (n)				

Extended Consonant Syllables

	A	I	U	E	O
G	が (ga)	ぎ (gi)	ぐ (gu)	げ (ke)	ご (go)
Z	ざ (za)	じ (ji)	ず (zu)	ぜ (ze)	ぞ (zo)
D	だ (da)	ぢ (ji)	づ (zu)	で (de)	ど (do)
B	ば (ba)	び (bi)	ぶ (bu)	べ (be)	ぼ (bo)
P	ぱ (pa)	ぴ (pi)	ぷ (pu)	ぺ (pe)	ぽ (po)

Modified Syllables or Digraphs

Some Hiragana characters are combined with 'ya', 'yu', or 'yo' to extend Japanese sounds and are called digraphs. In such combinations, the first Hiragana is written in its normal size while the second one is written in a smaller size.

YA	YU	YO
きゃ kya	きゅ kyu	きょ kyo
ぎゃ gya	ぎゅ gyu	ぎょ gyo
しゃ sha	しゅ shu	しょ sho
じゃ ja	じゅ ju	じょ jo
ちゃ cha	ちゅ chu	ちょ cho
ぢゃ ja	ぢゅ ju	ぢょ jo
にゃ nya	にゅ nyu	にょ nyo
ひゃ hya	ひゅ hyu	ひょ hyo
びゃ bya	びゅ byu	びょ byo
ぴょ pyo	ぴゅ pyu	ぴょ pyo
みゃ mya	みゅ my	みょ myo
りゃ rya	りゅ ryu	りょ ryo

Vowels

Italian and Spanish speakers will find that Japanese vowels have similar sounds as Italian and Spanish vowels.

In Japanese, each vowel produces a distinct sound. They are pronounced separately and do not blend together when placed beside each other.

Vowel	Approximate English Sound
あ (a)	like the "a" in father
い (i)	like the "e" in meat
う (u)	like the "oo" in food
え (e)	like the "e" in egg
お (o)	like the "o" in old

Long Vowel Sound

The long vowel sound is produced by prolonging a vowel sound's duration. This is done by appending one of the characters 「う」, 「い」, or 「あ」 to the appropriate vowel as indicated by the following chart:

Vowel sound	Extended by
あ (a)	あ
い (i), え (e)	い
う (u), お (o)	う

Examples:

せんせい -> sen-sē -> teacher

がくせい -> ga-ku-sē -> student

11

おかあさん -> o-kā-san -> mother

おはよう -> o-ha yō -> good morning

きょう -> kyō -> today

Take note, however, of some exceptions. In some words, the vowel sound /e/ is prolonged by adding 「え」 and the vowel sound /o/ is prolonged by appending 「お」.

Here are examples of these exceptions:

おねえさん -> o-nē-san -> sister

おおい -> ōi -> cover

おおきい -> ōkī -> big

Pronunciation Guide

The Hiragana は is pronounced "ha" only when it is used within a word. When placed immediately after the topic of a sentence, it is pronounced as "wa".

With the exception of 「ん」, 「ち」, 「し」, and 「つ」, you'll have an idea how each character sounds by combining the consonant with the vowel. Take note of the sounds however that don't conform to the basic consonant-vowel sound, namely: し (shi), ち (chi), つ (tsu), ふ (fu), and ん (n).

The Japanese /r/ sound is quite unlike any English sound. It is produced by hitting the roof of your mouth with your tongue.

The 「ん」 character has no vowel sound and is rarely used by itself. It is commonly used with another character to add the /n/ sound. For example, it can be added to 「ま」 (ma) to form 「まん」 (man) or to 「か」 (ka) to form 「かん」 (kan).

You must learn the correct direction and stroke order for each character.

Hiragana	Romaji	English Translation
わたし	watashi	I (formal: males/normal: females)
ぼく	boku	I (normal: males)
かれ	kare	he
かのじょ	kanojo	she
あなた	anata	you (singular/normal)
ここ	koko	here
それ	sore	that (noun)
これ	kore	this (noun)
この	kono	this (demonstrative)
その	sono	that (demonstrative)
そこ	soko	there
ひと	hito	person
いえ	ie	house
ねこ	neko	cat
いぬ	inu	dog
ありがとう ございます	arigatou gozaimasu	Thank you. (formal)
ありがとう	arigatou	Thank you. (normal)
どういたしまして	douitashimashite	You're welcome. (normal)
おはようございます	ohayou gozaimasu	Good morning. (normal/formal)
おはよう	ohayou	Good morning. (informal)
さよなら	sayonara	Goodbye. (normal)
こんばんは	konbanwa	Good evening. (normal)
こんにちは	konnichiwa	Hello. (normal)
きをつけてください	ki o tsukete kudasai	Take care. Be careful
がんばってください	gambatte kudasai	Hang in there.

Katakana カタカナ

Katakana is primarily used for foreign loan words and is the least frequently used script. It represents the same phonetic sounds used in Hiragana but are written in different character sets.

When creating a name equivalent in Katakana, it must sound like its closest equivalent in Japanese sound.

	A	I	U	E	O
	ア a	イ i	ウ u	エ e	オ o
K	カ ka	キ ki	ク ku	ケ ke	コ ko
	ガ ga	ギ gi	グ gu	ゲ ge	ゴ go
S	サ sa	シ shi	ス su	セ se	ソ so
	ザ za	ジ ji	ズ zu	ゼ ze	ゾ zo
T	タ ta	チ chi	ツ tsu	テ te	ト to
	ダ da	ヂ ji	ヅ zu	デ de	ド do
N	ナ na	ニ ni	ヌ nu	ネ ne	ノ no
H	ハ ha	ヒ hi	フ fu	ヘ he	ホ ho
	バ ba	ビ bi	ブ bu	ベ be	ボ bo
	パ pa	ピ pi	プ pu	ペ pe	ポ po
M	マ ma	ミ mi	ム mu	メ me	モ mo
Y	ヤ ya		ユ yu		ヨ yo
R	ラ ra	リ ri	ル ru	レ re	ロ ro
W	ワ wa	ヲ wo	ン n/m		

Long Vowel Sound

Long vowels that come after a consonant are denoted by a dash symbol after the character.

Examples:

ツアー -> tsu-ā -> tour

メール -> mē -ru -> email

ケーキ -> kē-ki -> cake
コーヒー -> kōhī -> coffee

Japanese Loan Words: Gairaigo (外来語)

Except for words of Chinese origins, most borrowed words are written in Katakana. They are pronounced using Japanese rules for pronunciation and syllabication. Many are even abbreviated. Hence, the original foreign word is hardly recognizable.

Here are examples of loan words:

ビル -> biru -> building

スーパー -> suupaa -> supermarket

デパート -> depaato -> department store

イラスト -> irasuto -> illustration

メーク -> meeku -> make-up

ダイヤ -> daiya -> diamond

マイク -> maiku -> microphone

Multiple words may likewise be abbreviated to a few syllables such as the following:

エアコン -> eakon -> air conditioning

ワープロ -> waapuro -> word processor

パソコン -> pasokon -> personal computer

コンビ -> konbini -> convenience store

マスコミ -> masukomi -> mass media (mass communication)

プロレス -> puroresu -> professional wrestling

アメフト -> Amefuto -> American football

Words of foreign origin are typically assimilated into Japanese as nouns. When combined with the irregular verb "suru", the loan word becomes a verb.

Examples:

ノックする -> nokku suru -> to knock

キスする -> kisu suru -> to kiss

タイプする -> taipu suru -> to type

ドライブする -> doraibu suru -> to drive

Here are other commonly used loan words:

アイドル	aidoru	pop star, idol
アイスクリーム	aisukuriimu	ice cream
アニメ	anime	animation
アンケート	ankeeto	questionnaire/survey (French enquete)
アルバイト	arubaito	part-time job (German arbeit)
バー	baa	bar
バーゲン	baagen	a store sale (from bargain)

バター	bataa	butter
ビール	biiru	beer
ボールペン	booru pen	ballpoint pen
ドラマ	dorama	TV drama
エンジン	enjin	engine
エレベーター	erebeetaa	elevator
フライ	furai	deep frying
フロント	furonto	reception desk
ガム	gamu	chewing gum
ガラス	garasu	glass
ゴム	gomu	rubber band (Dutch gom)
ハンドル	handoru	handle
ハンカチ	hankachi	handkerchief
ホテル	hoteru	hotel
イメージ	imeeji	image
ジュース	juusu	juice
カメラ	kamera	camera
カレンダー	karendaa	calendar
コック	kokku	cook
マッチ	macchi	match
ミシン	mishin	sewing machine

レジ	reji	cash register
レストラン	resutoran	restaurant
ルール	ruuru	rule
スマート	sumaato	smart
スタイル	sutairu	style
ストーリー	sutoorii	story
テレビ	terebi	television
トンネル	tonneru	tunnel

Expressing Nationality

A person's nationality is expressed by simply adding 人 jin (person) after the name of the country.

Examples:

アメリカ人 -> Amerika-jin -> American

カナダ人 -> Kanada-jin -> Canadian

オランダ人 -> Oranda-jin -> Dutch

フランス人 -> Furansu-jin -> French

ドイツ人 -> Doitsu-jin -> Germany

イタリア人 -> Itaria-jin -> Italian

スペイン人 -> Supein-jin -> Spanish

Kanji

Kanji is a set of Chinese characters that were adopted by the Japanese in the 5th century. Kanji characters are ideograms. Each character conveys its own meaning instead of merely representing phonetics.

Almost all Japanese nouns as well as stems of verbs and adjectives are written in Kanji. Adverbs are also often written in Kanji. Hence, to be able to read most Japanese words, you will have to learn Kanji. There are 2,136 characters that have been officially identified as commonly used kanji and these are the ones being taught at schools in Japan. There are thousand other kanji characters that are being used by highly literate people. Native Japanese speakers and students take years to learn kanji. You can start learning them by familiarizing yourself with the most commonly used kanji in conversational Japanese.

Here are some of the most frequently used kanji:

Kanji	Meaning	Kanji	Meaning
事	affair, matter	今	now
後	after	一	one
飛行機	airplane	自	oneself
酒	alcohol	対	opposite
前	before	人	people, human being
自転車	bicycle	民	people, nation
大	big	相	phase, mutual
体	body	場	place
本	book	党	political party

明	bright, clear	力	power
京	capital	問	question
子	child	実	real
市	city	雨	rain
社	company, society	米	rice
国	country	田	rice field
氏	courtesy name (Mr., Mrs.)	正	right, correct
度	degree, time	川	river
方	direction	同	same
下	down, under	部	section
東	east	七	seven
八	eight	六	six
目	eye	小	small
電	electricity	日	sun
少	few	寿司	sushi
野	field	十	ten
五	five	万	ten thousand
火	fire	三	three
魚	fish	時	time
四	four	合	to combine

政	government, politics	食べる	to eat
地	ground, place	入	to enter
手	hand	表	to express, surface
和	harmonious, peace	定	to fix
心	heart	行	to go
高	high, expensive	出	to go out
家	house	保	to keep, to maintain
安	inexpensive, peaceful	会	to meet
内	inside	動	to move
間	interval, between	開	to open
日本	Japan	言	to say
文	letter, writings	見	to see, to look
生	life	話	to speak
長	long	立	to stand
主	main, master	発	to start, to emit
男	man	学	to study
多	many	代	generation, to substitute

中	middle	思	to think
意	mind, meaning	回	to turn around, time
分	minute	二	two
金	money, gold	上	up, top
月	month, moon	水	water
山	mountain	道	way
新	new	全	whole
九	nine	女	woman
北	north	年	year
不	not, un~, in~	円	Yen (Japanese currency)

Stroke Order

Learning the proper stroke order and direction is extremely important when learning kanji.

Strokes generally begin from the top left corner toward the bottom right. Hence, when writing vertical strokes, you'll have to start from the top going down to the bottom part. Horizontal strokes, on the other hand, are written from left to right.

Kanji Radicals

Every Kanji contains one classifying radical. Each radical has at least one meaning and it imparts this meaning to the kanji. Familiarizing yourself with radicals can help you learn to decipher the meaning of unknown kanji. As most kanjis are classified in dictionaries based on their radicals (Bushu index), the ability to recognize the radical is essential if you want lto look up a kanji in a dictionary.

In the following examples, the three kanjis have similar right part. Their left part, however, is different from each other. This part is the kanji's radical.

時 -> This kanji's radical is 日 which can mean time, day, or sun while the kanji stands for "time".

詩 -> This kanji's radical is 言 which can mean say, to speak, or words while the kanji stands for "poem or poetry".

持 -> This kanji's radical is 扌 which means hand while the kanji means "to hold".

There are 214 radicals in Japanese kanji and they form the Bushu index. A radical can appear anywhere in a character. They are grouped into seven categories based on their position. Take note that some kanji are radicals by themselves (大, 月, 日) which makes their position irrelevant. Hence, they don't belong to any category.

Categories of Radicals Based on their Position with the Kanji

つくり -> tsukuri -> right side radicals

へん -> hen -> left side radicals

かんむり -> kanmuri -> top radicals

あし -> ashi -> bottom radicals

たれ -> tare -> hang-down radicals

かまえ -> kamae -> enclosing radicals

にょう -> nyou -> bottom-wrapping radicals

Kanji Pronunciation

A kanji typically has more than one pronunciation The on'yomi 音読み or ON readings are based on Chinese pronunciation while the kun'yomi 訓読み or KUN readings are based on the indigenous Japanese pronunciation.

Here are examples of kanji with dual readings:

English	Kanji	On'yomi	Kun'yomi
country	国	こく (ko ku)	くに (kuni)
dog	犬	けん (ken)	いぬ (inu)
eye	目	もく (mo ku)	め (me)
fire	火	か (ka)	ひ (hi)
inside	内	ない (nai)	うち (uchi)
man	男	だん (da n)	おとこ (o toko)
mountain	山	さん (san)	やま (yama)
tree	木	もく (mo ku)	き(ki)
water	水	すい (sui)	みず (mizu)
woman	女	じょ (ji ~yo)	おんな (on'na)

Although they are more the exception, there are kanji that take only one pronunciation either in on'yomi or kun'yomi.

Here are examples of Kanji with single on'yomi reading:

English	Kanji	On'yomi
doctor	医	い (i)
elephant	象	ぞう (zō)
feeling	感	かん (kan)
lumber	材	ざい (zai)
meat	肉	にく (niku)
second	秒	びょう (byō)
stomach	胃	い (i)
tea	茶	ちゃ (cha)
work	職	しょく (shoku)

On the other hand, some kanji characters only have kun'yomi pronunciation. These kanji were created in Japan to represent concepts that were indigenous to the country. They are referred to as 国字 Kokuji (national characters).

Here are examples of kanji with exclusively kun'yomi readings:

English	Kanji	Kun'yomi
field	畑	はたけ (hatake)
fragrant	匂い	におい (nioi)
frame	枠	わく (waku)
horse chestnut	栃	とち (to chi)
mountain pass	峠	とうげ (tō-ge)
princess	姫	ひめ (hime)
sardine	鰯	いわし (iwashi)
to be crowded	込む	こむ (komu)
to bloom	咲く	さく (saku)
unhulled rice	籾	もみ (momi)

Chapter 2: Basic Japanese Grammar

Word Order

In English, the basic sentence pattern is subject-verb-object. Japanese sentences follow a different word order where the verb is always placed at the end of a sentence. In some cases, the verb may be followed by a small word called particle. These particles are widely used in Japanese language to indicate the grammatical function of each sentence element.

A basic Japanese sentence is formed using the following pattern:

Topic / Subject + Object + Verb

To illustrate, here's a simple Japanese sentence:

わたしはさしみをたべる。

Watashi wa sashimi wo taberu.

I eat sashimi.

Notice that there are no spaces between characters or words in the sentence. The particles will usually tell you the point where a word ends. In the above example, there are two particles: は wa and をwo. The particle は wa indicates the topic or subject of the sentence while the particle をwo indicates the direct object. These particles come after the word they identify.

Let's analyze the parts of the sentence.

わたし -> Watashi -> subject

は -> wa

さしみ -> sashimi -> sashimi -> direct object

を -> wo

たべる -> taberu -> eat -> verb

Native Japanese speakers will usually drop the personal pronoun when talking about themselves. Hence, you'll probably hear this:

さしみをたべる。 -> Sashimi wo taberu.

In English, this is translated literally as "Sashimi eat."

In informal conversations, the particle をwo is commonly omitted. Hence, you'll frequently hear native speakers say:

さしみたべる。 -> Sashimi taberu.

Using the basic pattern, you can form other simple sentences like the following:

わたしはおちゃをのむ。 -> I drink tea.

Watashi wa ocha wo nomu

わたしはテレビをみる。 -> I watch TV.

Watashi wa terebi wo miru

You can state your age following this simple sentence pattern. For example, to say that you are eighteen years old:

わたしは18さいです。

Watashi wa juhassai desu.

Adjective Placement

In Japanese, the adjective is placed before the word it modifies.

Examples:

おいしいすし -> Oishī sushi -> delicious sushi

かわいいおんなのこ -> kawaii onna-no-ko -> cute girl

To say that "Sushi is delicious", you will still follow the basic construction:

すしはおいしいです。 -> Sushi wa oishī desu. -> Sushi is delicious.

In the above sentence, "desu" is the verb "to be" and it is placed at the end of the sentence.

Adverb Placement

Adverbs of time and place can't be placed at the end of the sentence as this is the verb's rightful place. You may place them at the beginning of the sentence or before the verb.

Words that describe time are generally placed at the start of a sentence. The word order, in this case, will usually be:

<Time> + (subject) + Object + Verb

For example, to translate the statement "I will buy a new bag tomorrow", try to break it down into different parts:

To buy = かう kau

New = あたらしい atarashii

bag = バッグ baggu

tomorrow = あした ashita

あした、あたらしいバッグをかう。

Ashita, atarashī baggu wo kau.

Tomorrow, I will buy a new bag.

Words that indicate location can be placed at the beginning of the sentence.

For example, to say that you want to buy a new bag in the department store, here's how you can form the sentence:

To buy -> かう -> kau

New -> あたらしい -> atarashii

bag -> バッグ -> baggu

depaato -> デパート -> department store

デパートであたらしいバッグをかう。

Depaato de atarashī baggu wo kau.

I will buy a new bag at the department store.

Notice that the particle で (de) was placed after the word デパート (depaato) to indicate that this is the location of the action.

Time and Place Words in a Sentence

If a sentence has both Time and Place words, the Time word is generally placed before the Place word. Hence, if you want to say "I will buy a new bag in the department store tomorrow", here's how you would normally form the sentence:

あした、デパートであたらしいバッグをかう。

Ashita, depaato de atarashī baggu wo kau.

Tomorrow, I will buy a new bag at the department store.

Forming Simple Questions

In Japanese, you can turn a sentence into a question by just adding the particle か ka at the end of a noun sentence. The particle か ka is used to express the speaker's doubt, uncertainty, or question about something. Remember to raise your tone when you read the particle to indicate that you are asking a question.

For example, the following sentence states that Tom is a dancer:

トムはダンサーです。

Tomu wa dansā desu

To turn it into a question, you can add the particle か ka as follows:

トムはダンサーです**か**。

Tomu wa dansā desu ka.

Is Tom a dancer?

The question is a yes-no question. To reply, you can start the answer with either a yes - はい (ha i) or no - いいえ i i e.

For example, to say yes to the above question:

はい、トムはダンサーです

ha i Tomu wa dansā desu

Yes, tom is a dancer.

On the other hand, to say that no, Tom is not a dancer:

いいえ、トムはダンサーです

i i e Tomu wa dansā desu

No, Tom is not a dancer.

Take note that the Japanese words はい ha i and いいえ i i e are not exact translations of the English yes or no. The word はい ha i conveys that the speaker agrees with what the other person said while the word いいえ i i e conveys that the speaker does not agree with what the other person expressed.

Chapter 3: Particles

Particles 助詞 (joshi)

Particles are tiny words that indicate the relationship between words in a sentence. They are used after other words like nouns adjectives, and verbs. Some particles are comparable to English prepositions. There are 188 particles in Japanese.

Here are the main particles and their uses:

Particle	romanji	Usage
は	wa	topic marker
が	ga	subject marker
を	wo (pronounced "o")	direct object marker
へ	e	direction marker
に	ni	indirect object marker, time marker, direction marker

Particles は)wa and (が) ga: Topic Marker and Subject Marker

The particle (は) wa indicates the topic of the sentence while (が) ga specifies the subject. In Japanese, the topic may be the same as the subject of the sentence. They can also be different. In many cases, the topic can be implied and omitted.

The topic may refer to anything (location, object, or other grammatical elements) that the speaker wants to discuss. It can be likened to the expressions "Speaking of" or "As for".

For example:

私は学生です。　-> I am a student.

Watashi wa gakusei desu. -> As for me, I'm a student.

日本語は面白いです。　-> Japanese is interesting.

Nihongo wa omoshiroi desu. -> Speaking of Japanese, it is interesting.

The topic and the corresponding particle can be omitted from the sentence without changing its meaning. This is usually done when the topic is understood.

In the following example, you can drop the words inside the parenthesis without altering the idea:

(私は)ジョンです。　-> I am John.

(Watashi wa) Jon desu.

The particle が ga is used to introduce a new subject. Once the subject has been identified, the particle はwa is then used to specify the same subject in subsequent sentences.

For example:

昔，おじいさんが住んでいました。

Mukashi, ojii-san ga sunde imashita.

A long time ago, there lived an old man.

おじいさんはとても親切でした。

Ojii-san wa totemo shinsetsu deshita.

The old man was very kind.

The subject おじいさん ojii-san (old man) was mentioned for the first time in the first sentence. In the succeeding sentence, it became a topic and was specified with は wa.

The particle は wa is likewise used to emphasize the subject or show contrast.

The particle (が) ga is a much more straightforward particle than (は) wa. Its primary role is to indicate the subject of a sentence or clause. A noun marked with (が) ga is commonly associated with a verb which is properly inflected to indicate the noun's state of being or action.

Particle を (wo or o): Direct Object Marker

The particle を (wo or o) is used to mark the direct object in a Japanese sentence.

Example:

watashi wa kanojo wo ie ni okuru. -> I'm going to take her home.

The particle に (ni)

This particle is used to mark the direction, time or the indirect object in a sentence.

Examples:

In the following example, the 'ni' particle indicates the direction by functioning like the English preposition "to":

watashi wa kanojo wo ie ni okuru -> I'm going to take her (to) home.

The "ni" particle can likewise be used to indicate time.

For example:

watashi wa sanji ni hanareru -> I'm leaving at 3 o'clock.

Finally, the "ni" particle can be use to mark an indirect object.

Example:

watashi wa kare ni ie made okurareta -> I was taken home by him.

Take note that in all of the above examples, you can drop the "watashi wa" as it is already implied.

Sentence ending particles

There are several Japanese particles that are added at the end of a sentence. These particles are used to express the speaker's doubt, admiration, hesitation, caution, emphasis, doubt, etc. Some of the sentence-ending particles identify male or female speech.

Here are some of the most commonly used sentence-ending particles:

か **ka**

The particle "ka" transforms a sentence into a question.

日本人ですか。　-> Are you a Japanese?

Nihon-jin desu ka.

な **kana** / かしら **kashira**

The particles kana or kashira indicates uncertainty about something. You can translate is as "I wonder". The form kashira is used only by female speakers.

あの人は誰か しら。-> I wonder who that person is.

Ano hito wa dare kashira.

渡辺さんは今晩来るかな -> I wonder if Mr. Watanabe will come tonight.

Watanabe-san wa konban kuru kana

な na

The particle な na can be placed at the end of a sentence as a negative imperative marker to indicate prohibition. It is used by men in highly informal speech.

食べるな! -> Don't eat!

Taberu na

行くな! -> Don't go!

Ikuna!

そんなことをするな！ -> Don't do such thing!

Sonna koto o suru na!

It is also used to place casual emphasis on an opinion, suggestion, or decision.

これは間違っていると思うな。 -> I think this is wrong.

Kore wa machigatte iru to omou na.

なあ nā

The particle なあ nā can be used to express an emotion or wishful thinking.

すごいなあ。 -> How great it is!

Sugoi nā

もう少し寝ていたいなあ。 -> I wish I could sleep a little more.

Mō sukoshi nctc itai nā

ね ne

The particle ね ne is used at the end of a sentence to indicate that the speaker is seeking for the listener's confirmation It is the equivalent of English expressions like "right?", "isn't it?", or "don't you think so?"

いい天気ですね。 -> It's a beautiful day, isn't it?

Ī tenki desu ne.

The Particle の no

Expressing Possession with the particle の no

The particle の no is commony used to express possession in Japanese. When used after わたし watashi, it is translated as the English possessive pronoun "my".

Examples:

わたし の なまえ -> my name

watashi wo namae

わたしのともだち -> my friend

Watashi no tomodachi

It can also be used with other pronouns to indicate possession:

あなたの友達 -> your friend

anata no tomodachi

かれのともだち -> his friend

kare no tomodachi

かのじょのともだち -> her friend

kanoji ~yo no tomodachi

Expressing "at" or "of" with the particle の no

The particle の no is a flexible particle that can also be used to denote "at" or "of".

Example:

高校の先生 -> teacher of high school

Kōkō no sensei

Chapter 4: Nouns

Unlike other languages, Japanese nouns don't inflect. They mostly remain the same regardless of gender or number. However, they take particles to mark their place in a sentence.

There are no plural forms in Japanese. Plural words are usually marked by using a number and counter. They may also be made known through context. Some nouns indicate plurality through a pluralizing suffix while other nouns rely on repetition to express plurality.

Using Japanese Nouns to Express Present State of Being

A noun is a word that names a person, thing, event, place, or idea. They are used as subject, object, or complement. In Japanese, you can turn a noun into a sentence by simply adding だ da (I) or です desu (to be).

For example, to turn the name Louie into a sentence, you can attach one of the above hiragana characters to it:

るい -> Rui -> Louie

るいだ -> Rui da -> I'm Louie.

るいです -> Rui desu -> I'm Louie.

学生だ -> Gakusei da -> I'm a student.

学生です -> Gakusei desu -> I'm a student.

While だ (da) and です(desu) conveys similar meaning, there is a difference in nuance. The level of politeness can be expressed by adding a character at the end of a sentence. The character だ is commonly used in familiar Japanese while です is used in polite conversations. You can even drop だ in casual conversations. However, Japanese people use です when speaking to someone they have just met. Failing to do so will make them appear rude. As a new learner, it is best to practice polite expressions to create a good impression.

Expressing Present Negative State of Being

In Japanese, the negative is expressed through conjugation. You can conjugate a noun to say that someone or something is not X.

Instead of だ (da), you can attach じゃない (janai) to state the negative in casual conversations. For polite conversations, you can use じゃありません (ja arimasen) in place of だ.

For example, to state that you're not a student:

Informal -> 学生+じゃない = 学生じゃない。 -> Gakusei janai

Polite -> 学生+じゃありません = 学生じゃありません。 -> Gakusei ja arimasen

There is another level of politeness in negative forms and that is the polite colloquial. This is more often heard in conversations than in written Japanese. You can express it by adding です (desu) to じゃない (janai).

Hence:

Polite (colloquial) -> 学生 + じゃない + -> です。学生じゃないです。

When making a public speech, writing a letter, or talking with business partners, you can express a higher level of formality by replacing じゃ (ja) with では (dewa).

Examples:

Informal

学生 +ではない -> 学生ではない。 -> Gakusei dewa nai.

Polite

学生 +ではありません -> 学生ではありません。 -> Gakusei dewa arimasen

Polite (colloquial)

学生 +ではない+です -> 学生ではないです。 -> Gakusei dewa nai desu.

Expressing Past State of Being

To express that X was X, you can simply attach だった datta to either noun or a na-adjective.

Examples:

しょうぼうし+だった -> shōbō-shi + datta

しょうぼうしだった -> shōbō-shi data -> was a firefighter

彼氏 + だった -> kareshi + datta

彼氏 だった -> kareshi datta -> was a boyfriend

Take note that だった datta is the past form of だ (da) and is used in informal situations. Its polite form is でした (deshita).

Example:

しょうぼうし+ でした -> shōbō-shi + deshita

しょうぼうしでした -> shōbō-shi deshita -> was a firefighter

Expressing Negative Past State of Being

To express the negative past and indicate "was not", you will conjugate the present negative tense by dropping い (i) from じゃない janai and attaching かった katta.

Examples:

学生じゃなかった。 -> was not a student

Gakusei janakatta

友達じゃなかった -> was not a friend

Tomodachi janakatta

Modifying a Noun with another Noun

If you want to use a noun to describe another noun like "pizza of New York", you can do that with the particle の (no).

The structure for this noun usage is as follows:

Noun A の Noun B

When you use the above model, it can convey the following meanings:

Possession

Content

Belonging

Location

Nature/Attribution

- *Possession*

The sentence pattern indicates that Noun A possesses Noun B.

Examples:

わたしのバッグ

wa ta shi no baggu

My bag

ジョンさんのとけい

Jon san no tokei

John's watch

- *Content*

The same model can be used to describe a noun with the other noun by providing information about its content. In this case, Noun A describes the content of Noun B.

Examples:

ガーデニングのほん

Gādeningu no hon

Book of gardening

りかのきょうかしょ

rika no kyou ka sho

science textbook

- *Belonging*

In this case, Noun A is the name of the group, company, or organization to which Noun B belongs.

Example:

トヨタの従業員

Toyota no jūgyōin

A Toyota employee

- *Location*

In this usage, Noun B provides a more specific location relative to the location indicated by Noun A.

ストーブの上

sutōbu no ue

On top of the stove

とだなのなか

toda na no naka

Inside the cabinet

- *Attribution/Nature*

Noun A is used to describe the nationality or gender of Noun B, a person.

アメリカンのせんせい

Amerikan no sensei

American teacher

おんなのがくせい

on na no ga ku sei

female student

Chapter 5: Personal Pronouns

A pronoun is a word that replaces a noun. In most languages, pronouns perform a variety of grammatical functions and are widely used. Japanese has a variety of pronouns to reflect the style of speech or gender. These pronouns, however, are not as frequently used as their counterparts in English. Native Japanese speakers frequently prefer to drop the personal pronouns in their sentences when the context is clear. A grammatical subject is not a stringent requirement in Japanese sentences.

It is as important to learn how to use personal pronoun as it is to know when not to use them.

Singular Personal Pronouns

First Person

Depending on who you are addressing, following are the different ways to say the pronoun "I" in Japanese:

わたくし -> watakushi -> very formal

わたし -> watashi -> formal

僕 -> boku (male) -> informal

あたし -> atashi (female) -> informal

俺 -> ore (male) -> very informal

The pronoun "watakushi" is an extremely polite personal pronoun. It is used in official conversations by both men and women but more so by women.

The most commonly used first person personal pronoun is "watashi" and it is considered the standard first person pronoun. It is used by men and women but it sounds more formal when used by men. It it is more often dropped in conversations. It is a contracted form of the pronoun "watakushi".

The pronoun "boku" is a familiar pronoun commonly used by males. It is used to some extent by younger and tomboyish girls.

The personal pronoun "atashi" is a familiar pronoun used by younger women. It exudes cuteness and a youthful aura. It is mostly used in conversations and almost never used in written communication. It is somehow associated with geisha speech.

The pronoun 俺 "ore" is used in familiar situations by males. It is used when talking to family or friends.

Second Person

It is not uncommon for Japanese speakers to address the second person directly by their name. Many find it too direct or rude to use the word "you" when speaking directly to someone.

Here are the different forms of the personal pronoun "You" in Japanese:

おたく -> otaku -> very formal

あなた -> anata -> formal

君 -> kimi (male) -> informal

お前 -> omae (male) -> very informal

あんた -> anta -> very informal

The most commonly used second person personal pronoun is あなたー "anata" and it is a formal form. Like "watashi", it is frequently omitted. It is sometimes used to ask someone a question. It is better to avoid using "you" pronouns in Japanese if you know the person's name. The pronoun "anata" may also be used by wives when speaking to their husband in which case it takes on the meaning of "honey" or "dear".

The pronoun 君 "kimi" is commonly used when a male addresses a male friend in familiar situations. It is a familiar form of "you" which is more frequently used by males but may sometimes be used by girls. It may be used by people who are superior to others.

The pronoun あんた anta is a very familiar form of "you". It is used by parents to speak to their children in a stern voice. You can use this when talking on an angry tone to another person.

The pronoun お前 "omae" is a highly informal pronoun that is frequently used by males. It can be used to address someone in an insulting manner or when people are engaged in a fight. It can also be used, however, in situations that aren't rude such as when a husband addresses his wife, when a father talks to his children, when one is speaking to a pet, or when a teacher is addressing his student.

Third Person

The pronoun 彼 "kare" is frequently used to convey the third person personal pronoun "he" or "him" in formal situations. In many instances, the word "kare" is used to refer to a "boyfriend". To talk about a third person you're not familiar with, you can use "ano otoko" to mean "that man".

The pronoun 彼女 "kanojo" is often used to mean "girlfriend". It can be used to mean she or her in formal situations. To talk about a third person you're not familiar with, you can use "ano ko" to convey "that girl" or "that kid".

The words あの人 "ano hito" means "that person". It is used when you're not particular about the gender of the third person.

The pronoun あの方 "ano kata" is also translated as "that person" and is used in formal situations.

Plural Personal Pronouns

In general, the suffix たち (tachi) or ら (ra) is used to form plural nouns. Take note that nouns generally take on the same form regardless of number.

私たち -> Watashitachi -> we or us

彼ら -> Karera -> we/us – group of mixed genders or guys

彼女たち -> Kanojotachi -> we/us – group of girls

あなた達 -> Anatatachi -> you (plural) – familiar conversations

あなた方 -> Anatagata -> you (plural) – formal conversations

俺ら -> Orera -> we (group of men) – familiar conversations

Chapter 6: Demonstrative Pronouns and Adjectives

The words "this" and "that" are examples of demonstrative pronouns and demonstrative adjectives.

The words これ (kore), それ (sore), and あれ (are) are the most frequently used demonstrative pronouns in Japanese. They are used to refer to people or things around the speaker. Japanese demonstrative pronouns are not followed by a noun.

The Japanese language uses three demonstrative adjectives: この kono, その sono, and あの ano. Like their English counterparts, they are followed by a noun.

Demonstrative Pronouns

Following are the demonstrative pronouns and their uses:

これ -> kore -> used when talking about an object near the speaker

それ -> sore -> used when talking about an object near the listener

あれ -> are -> used when referring to an object far from the speaker an listener

Bear in mind that the type of demonstrative pronoun to be used is based on the speaker's point of view.

For example, the speaker can point to a book beside him and say:

これはわたしの**本**です。

kore wa watashi no hon desu

This is my book.

If the speaker points to a book beside the listener, he may say:

それはあなたの**本**です。

sore wa anata no hon desu

That is your book.

If the speaker points to a book that is quite distant from him and the speaker, he may say:

あれはジョンさんの**本**です。

are wa jon san no hon desu

That (over there) is John's book.

If the speaker and listener are standing closely together, they may speak as a single entity if the situation warrants. Hence, they may use これ (kore) to point to an object near them, それ (sore) to refer to an object that is slightly far from them, and あれ (are) to point to something that is quite distant from them.

Demonstrative Adjectives

A Japanese demonstrative adjective modifies the noun that comes after it. Here are the three demonstrative adjectives and their usage:

この Noun -> kono Noun -> points to a person or object near the speaker

その Noun -> sono Noun -> points to a person or object near the listener

あの Noun -> ano Noun -> points to a person or object distant from both speaker and listener

To illustrate using the same examples used in demonstrative pronouns, a speaker may refer to a book beside him and say:

この**本**はわたしのです。

kono hon wa watashi no desu

This book is mine.

The speaker may point to a book beside the listener and express:

その**本**はあなたのです。

sono hon wa anata no desu

That book is yours.

The speaker may refer to a book that is distant from both of them and express:

あの本はジョンさんのです。

ano hon wa jon san no desu

That book (over there) is John's.

If the speaker and listener are standing closely together, they may speak as a single entity if the situation warrants. Hence, they may use この Noun to point to a person or object near them, その Noun to refer to a person or object that is slightly far from them, and あの Noun to point to a person or object that is quite distant from them.

Demonstrative Pronouns (Places)

The demonstrative pronouns ここ koko, そこ soko, and あそこ asoko are used when referring to places.

ここ -> koko -> specifies the place where the speaker is located

そこ -> soko -> indicates the place where the listener is located

あそこ -> asoko -> specifies a place that is distant from both speaker and listener

When the speaker considers that he/she is sharing the same place as the speaker, the pronoun ここ koko is used to indicate the place where they are both located. The pronoun そこ soko is used to indicate a location that is slightly distant from both of them. The pronoun あそこ asoko is used to refer to a more distant place.

There is another group of demonstrative pronouns that can be used to describe places as well as point somebody to a certain direction. The following forms for demonstrative pronouns are considered more polite than koko, soko, and asoko:

こちら -> kochira

そちら -> sochira

あちら -> achira

Chapter 7: Verbs

Japanese verbs are generally found at the end of a sentence. Since the subject is frequently omitted, the verb plays a critical role in making the sentence understandable.

While Japanese verb forms are considerably difficult to learn, language learners have fewer rules to memorize when it comes to conjugation. Japanese verbs do not have separate forms to indicate the person, gender, or number of the subject.

Verbs are divided into three groups based on their basic or dictionary form.

Group 1: Verbs Ending in ~u

This verb group is also known as Godan-doushi (Godan verbs) or Consonant stem verbs. All Group 1 verbs end in –u.

Examples:

話す -> hanasu -> to speak

書く -> kaku -> to write

聞く -> kiku -> to listen

待つ -> matsu -> to wait

飲む -> nomu -> to drink

Group 2: Verbs Ending in ~ iru and ~ eru

Group 2 verbs are also known as Ichidan-doushi (Ichidan verbs) or Vowel-stem-verbs. A verb in this group ends with either "~iru" or "~ eru".

Examples:

着る -> kiru -> to wear

見る -> miru -> to see

起きる -> okiru -> to get up

降りる -> oriru -> to get off

信じる -> shinjiru -> to believe

開ける -> akcru -> to open

あげる -> ageru -> to give

出る -> deru -> to go out

寝る -> neru -> to sleep

食べる -> taberu -> to eat

Though the following verbs end in either –eru or –iru, they all belong to Group 1 verbs:

入る -> hairu -> to enter

走る -> hashiru -> to run

いる -> iru -> to need

帰る -> kaeru -> to return

限る -> kagiru -> to limit

切る -> kiru -> to cut

ゃべる -> shaberu -> to chatter

知る -> shiru -> to know

Group 3: Irregular Verbs

The verbs suru (to do) and kuru (to come) are the only irregular verbs in Japanese.

The verb "suru" is used to express the meaning "to make", "to do", or "to cost". It is the most frequently used Japanese verb. It is paired with various nouns to turn them into verbs.

Examples:

勉強する -> benkyousuru -> to study

ダンスする -> dansusuru -> to dance

シャンプーする -> shanpuusuru -> to shampoo

旅行する -> ryokousuru -> to travel

輸出する -> yushutsusuru -> to export

Conjugating Japanese Verbs

All Japanese verbs end with "u". This is the basic verb form that you will find in dictionaries. It is also the informal present affirmative verb form commonly used among family members and close friends in informal situations.

Conjugating Verbs to their Formal Verb Form

To make sentences polite, you will have to add the suffix "~masu to the basic verb from. This suffix only changes the tone from informal to polite or formal and has no specific meaning. The

"~masu verb form is used when the situation requires a degree of formality or politeness. It is the more suitable form for general use.

To demonstrate, here are the ~masu form of different verbs from the three verb groups:

Group 1 Verbs

To conjugate Group 1 verbs to its formal form, drop the final –u and add –imasu.

Examples:

      Informal -> Formal -> Meaning

話す -> hanasu -> hanasimasu -> to speak

書く -> kaku -> kakimasu -> to write

聞く -> kiku -> kikimasu -> to listen

待つ -> matsu -> matsimasu -> to wait

飲む -> nomu -> nomimasu -> to drink

Group 2 Verbs

To conjugate Group 2 Verbs to their formal verb form, drop the final ~ru and add ~ masu.

Examples:

      Basic -> Formal

着る -> kiru -> kimasu -> to wear

見る -> miru -> mimasu -> to see

信じる -> shinjiru -> shinjimasu -> to believe

開ける -> akeru -> akemasu -> to open

寝る -> neru -> nemasu -> to sleep

食べる -> taberu -> tabemasu -> to eat

Group 3 Verbs

To conjugate irregular verbs to their formal verb forms, the verb stem will have to change.

Examples:

する -> suru -> shimasu -> to do

来る -> kuru -> kimasu -> to come

Verb Stem

The stem of the verb is what's left after dropping the suffix –masu from the –masu form of the verb. Verb suffixes are attached to verb stems to convey different meanings.

Examples:

~ Masu Form -> Verb Stem

hanasimasu -> hanasi

kakimasu -> kaki

nomimasu -> nomi

kimasu -> ki

mimasu -> mi

tabemasu -> tabe

Present and Past Tenses

Japanese verbs have two principal tenses: the present and past tenses. The present tense is used to express habitual actions as well as future actions. There is no future tense in Japanese.

Present Tense

The informal present form of Japanese verbs is the same as its basic form which you have learned in the preceding lessons of this chapter. Similarly, the formal present form of the verbs is its – masu form.

Past Tense

The past form of Japanese verbs is used to denote past actions (I wrote, I played) as well as the present perfect tense (I have written, I have played).

Past Tense – Group 1 Verbs

Group 1 verbs are conjugated differently based on the basic form's last syllable consonant.

Past Tense - Informal Verb Form

Group 1 verbs are conjugated to its informal past form using the following rules:

Verb ending:

-ku   replace –ku with –ita   kaku > kaita (to write)

                                        kiku > kiita (to listen)

-gu   replace –gu with –ida   oyogu > oyoida (to swim)

                                          isogu > isoida (to hurry)

-u, -ru, and –tsu   replace ending with –tta   kaeru > kaetta (to return)

matsu > matta (to wait)

utau > utatta (to sing)

-bu, -mu, -nu   replace ending ith –nda   nomu > nonda

asobu > asonda (to play)

shinu > shinda (to die)

-su   replace –su with –shita   dasu > dashita (to take out)

hanasu > hanashita (to speak)

Past Tense – Formal Verb Form

To conjugate Group 1 verbs to their formal past tense form, drop the –u ending and add –imashita.

Examples:

nomu > nomimashita

kaku > kakimashita

kiku > kikimashita

Past Tense – Group 2 Verbs

Group 2 verbs follow the same conjugation pattern to form the past tense.

Past Tense – Informal Verb Form

To form the informal past tense for Group 2 verbs, drop –ru and add –ta.

Examples:

taberu > tabeta

miru > mita

Past Tense – Formal Verb Form

To form the formal past tense for Group 2 verbs, drop –ru and add mashita.

Examples:

taberu > tabemashita

miru > mimashita

Past Tense – Group 3 Verbs

Past Tense – Informal Verb Form

suru > shita

kuru > kita

Past Tense – Formal Verb Form

suru > shimashita

kuru > kimashita

Present Negative Forms

Present Negative – Informal Verb Form

To make negative sentences, you will have to replace the verb ending with the –nai suffix to form the negative.

Group 1 Verbs

To form the informal present negative for Group 1 verbs, drop the –u ending and add –anai. If the –u ending is preceded bya vowel, replace the vowel and –u with –wanai.

Examples:

nomu > nomanai

kiku > kikanai

au > awanai

Group 2 Verbs

To form the informal negative for Group 2 Verbs, drop the –ru ending and replace it with –nai.

Examples:

taberu > tabenai

miru > minai

Group 3 Verbs

Group 3 verbs take the following informal negative form:

suru > shinai

kuru > konai

Present Negative – Formal Verb Forms

To form the formal negative for all verb forms, simply replace the –masu ending with –masen.

Examples:

tabemasu > tabemasen

nomimasu > nomimasen

nemasu > nemasen

shimasu > shimasen

kimasu > kimasen

Past Negative Forms

Past Negative – Informal Verb Forms

To conjugate verbs to their informal past negative form, simply replace the –nai ending with –nakatta for all verb groups.

Examples:

nomanai > nomanakatta

kikanai > kikanakatta

awanai > awanakatta

tabenai > tabenakatta

minai > minakatta

shinai > shinakatta

konai > konakatta

Past Negative – Formal Verb Forms

To conjugate verbs to their formal past negative form, add "deshita" to their formal present negative form.

Examples:

tabemasen > tabemasen deshita

nomimasen > nomimasen deshita

nemasen > nemasen deshita

shimasen > shimasen deshita

kimasen > kimasen deshita

Most Commonly Used Japanese Verbs

Kana	Romaji	Kanji	English
あびる	abiru	浴びる	to take a shower
あげる	ageru		to give
あける	akeru	開ける	to open
あく	aku	開く	to open

あらう	arau	洗う	to wash
ある	aru	有る	to exist, to be
ある	aru	ある	to possess
あるく	aruku	歩く	to walk
あそぶ	asobu	遊ぶ	to play
あう	au	会う	to meet
ちがう	chigau	違う	to be different
だす	dasu	出す	to take out
でかける	dekakeru	出かける	to go out
できる	dekiru	出来る	can do
でる	deru	出る	to leave
ふく	fuku	吹く	to blow (wind)
ふる	furu	降る	to fall (snow, rain)
はいる	hairu	入る	to enter
はじまる	hajimaru	始まる	to begin
はく	haku	履く	to put on shoes
はなす	hanasu	話す	to speak, tell
はれる	hareru	晴れる	to clear up
はる	haru	張る	to stick or put something on
はしる	hashiru	走る	to run
はたらく	hataraku	働く	to work

ひく	hiku	引く	to pull
ひく	hiku	弾く	to play an instrument
いく	iku	行く	to go
いれる	ireru	入れる	to put in, insert
いる	iru		need,
いる	iru		to exist
いう	iu	言う	to tell/say
かぶる	kaburu	冠る	to put on a hat
かえる	kaeru	帰る	to return home
かえす	kaesu	返す	to return an object
かかる	kakaru		to take time or money
かける	kakeru		to wear
かける	kakeru		to place a phone call
かく	kaku	書く	to write
かりる	kariru	借りる	to borrow
かす	kasu	貸す	to lend
かう	kau	買う	to buy
けす	kesu	消す	to turn/switch off
きえる	kieru	消える	to vanish, go out
きく	kiku	聞く	to listen
きる	kiru	切る	to cut

きる	kiru	着る	to wear
こまる	komaru	困る	to be in trouble
こたえる	kotaeru	答える	to answer
くる	kuru	来る	to come
まがる	magaru	曲がる	to turn
まつ	matsu	待つ	to wait
みがく	migaku	磨く	to brush, polish
みる	miru	見る	to watch, see
みせる	miseru	見せる	to show
もつ	motsu	持つ	to own, to have
なく	naku	鳴く	to sing, moo, mew
ならべる	naraberu	並べる	to line up
ならぶ	narabu	並ぶ	to form a line
なる	naru		to become
ねる	neru	寝る	to sleep
のぼる	noboru	登る	to climb up
のむ	nomu	飲む	to drink
のる	noru	乗る	to ride/take
ぬぐ	nugu	脱ぐ	to take off clothes
おぼえる	oboeru	覚える	to remember/memorize
おきる	okiru	起きる	to stand up/get up

おく	oku		to put
おくる	okuru	送る	to send
おりる	oriru	降りる	to get off
おす	osu	押す	to push
おわる	owaru	終わる	to end
およぐ	oyogu	泳ぐ	to swim
さく	saku	咲く	to blossom
さす	sasu		to open an umbrella
しまる	shimaru	閉まる	to close
しめる	shimeru	閉める	to close
しめる	shimeru	締める	to fasten a belt
しぬ	shinu	死ぬ	to pass away, die
しる	shiru	知る	to know
すむ	sumu	住む	to reside
する	suru	する	to do
すう	suu	吸う	to smoke or breathe
すわる	suwaru	座る	to sit
たべる	taberu	食べる	to eat
たのむ	tanomu	頼む	to request/ask
たつ	tatsu	立つ	to stand
とぶ	tobu	飛ぶ	to fly
とまる	tomaru	止まる	to stop

とる	toru	取る	to take
とる	toru	撮る	to take a picture
つかれる	tsukareru	疲れる	to get tired
つかう	tsukau	使う	to use
つける	tsukeru	点ける	to turn on
つく	tsuku	着く	to arrive
つくる	tsukuru	作る	to produce/make
つとめる	tsutomeru	勤める	to work for someone
うまれる	umareru	生まれる	to be born
うる	uru	売る	to sell
うたう	utau	歌う	to sing
わかる	wakaru	分かる	to understand, to know
わすれる	wasureru	忘れる	to forget
わたる	wataru	渡る	to cross
わたす	watasu	渡す	to hand over
やる	yaru		to do
やすむ	yasumu	休む	to rest
よぶ	yobu	呼ぶ	to call
よむ	yomu	読む	to read

Chapter 8: Adjectives

An adjective is used to describe a noun. Japanese adjectives can be used to directly modify a noun that comes after it. Like nouns, they can also be connected using particles.

Japanese adjectives can be used as noun modifiers and predicates.

There are two categories of adjectives:

- い i-adjectives.

- な na-adjectives

I-adjectives end with い while na-adjectives are those that mostly don't end in い.

Adjectives as Noun Modifiers

Japanese adjectives are used to modify nouns. Adjectives used as noun modifiers take the basic form and are placed before the noun they describe. For なna-adjectives, however, you will have to add な na before the noun.

Here's the pattern:

Topic は い-adjective Noun です -> Topic wa i-adjective Noun desu

Topic は な-adjective な Noun です -> Topic wa na-adjective na Noun desu

Both patterns indicate that "Topic is an i/na-adjective Noun".

Examples:

I-adjectives

高い時計

takai tokei

expensive watch

小さい犬

chiisai inu

small dog

アキさんはやさしいひとです。

Aki-san wa yasashī hito desu

Mr. Aki is a kind person.

Na-adjectives

好きな映画

sukina eiga

favorite movie

78

有名な画家

yuumeina gaka

famous painter

彼は静かな人です。

Kare wa shizukana hito desu

He is a quiet person.

Forming Negative Adjectives

To conjugate an い-adjective to negative, drop the "い" and replace it with ない (nai) as shown in the following pattern:

い-adj(〜い)です to い-adj(〜くない)です

This form is commonly used in informal situations.

To convey formality, the negative form may be expressed by replacing "い" with ありません (arimasen) as indicated by the following pattern:

い-adj(〜い)です to い-adj(〜くありません)

To conjugate a な-adjective to its negative, drop です (desu) and replace it with ではありません (de wa arimasen) as indicated by this pattern:

な-adjです to な-adjではありません

Examples:

彼は静かな人ありません。 -> He is not a famous person.

Kare wa shizukana hito arimasen.

Adjectives as Predicate

When used as predicate, adjectives function as verbs. The pattern can be as simple as:

* Noun は い-adjective です -> Noun wa i-adjective desu

* Noun は な-adjective です -> Noun wa na-adjective desu

This translates to "Noun is adjective".

Examples:

アキさんはやさしいです。

Aki-san wa yasashī desu

Mr. Aki is friendly.

80

この車は高い

kono kuruma wa takai

This car is expensive.

Take note that when used as predicate, an adjective takes on the meaning "is friendly" or "is expensive" and not just "friendly" or"expensive". When used as predicate, i-adjectives may have to be followed by です"desu" to inject formality.

When they function as a verb, adjectives are also conjugated like verbs. The conjugation differs for i-adjectives and na-adjectives.

I-adjectives used as Predicate

Informal

In informal usage, i-adjectives take on the following forms for the present negative, past, and past negative:

Present Negative -> drop the i-ending and add –ku nai

Past -> drop the i-ending and add –katta

Past Negative -> drop the i-ending and add –ku nakatta

For example, here's how the adjective 高い takai (expensive) will be conjugated in informal usage:

Present -> 高い takai -> is expensive

Present negative -> 高くない takaku nai -> is not expensive

Past -> 高かった takakatta -> was expensive

Past Negative -> 高くなかった takaku nakatta -> was not expensive

この時計は高い。

Kono tokei wa takai -> This watch is expensive.

この時計は高くない。

Kono tokei wa takaku nai -> This watch is not expensive.

この時計は高かった。

Kono tokei wa takakatta -> This watch was expensive.

この時計は高くなかった。

Kono tokei wa takaku nakatta -> This watch was not expensive.

Formal

To convey formality, you can add desu to the informal forms.

To convey a slightly higher level of politeness in the adjective's negative forms, the adjective can take the following forms:

Present Negative -> drop the i-ending and add –ku arimasen

Past Negative -> drop the i-endinga and add –ku arimasen and – deshita

To demonstrate, here's how you would conjugate the adjective 高い takai to its formal forms:

Present -> 高いです takai desu

Present Negative -> 高くないですtakaku nai desu (formal)

高くありません takaku arimasen (slightly more formal)

Past -> 高かったですtakakatta desu

Past Negative -> 高くなかったですtakaku nakatta desu (formal)

高くありませんでした takaku arimasen deshita (slightly more formal)

Exception

Take note of the only exception to the conjugation of i-adjectives, the adjective いい "ii" which means "good". This adjective is derived from "yoi" and it is conjugated for the most part like "yoi".

The adjective いい "ii" takes the following informal and formal forms:

Informal

Present -> いい ii -> is good

Present Negative -> 良くない yoku nai -> is not good

Past -> 良かった yokatta -> was good

Past Negative -> 良くなかった yoku nakatta -> was not good

Formal

Present -> いいです ii desu

Present Negative -> 良くないです yoku nai desu (formal)

良くありません yoku arimasen (slightly more formal)

Past -> 良かったです yokatta desu

Past Negative -> 良くなかったです yoku nakatta desu (formal)

良くありませんでした yoku arimasen deshita (slightly more formal)

Na-adjectives Used as Predicate

Na-adjectives are made by a "~ na" ending when used as noun modifiers. Unlike i-adjectives, you can't use their basic adjective directly as predicates. You will have to drop the –na ending and add either –da (informal) or –desu (formal). Like when used with nouns, –da or –desu has to change their form to express the affirmative, negative, and the past.

Informal

In informal usage, the word 有名 yuumei (famous) takes the following forms to express the present, present negative, past, and past negative:

Present -> 有名だ yuumei da -> is famous

Present Negative -> 有名ではない yuumei dewa nai -> is not famous

Past -> 有名だった yuumei data -> was famous

Past Negative -> 有名ではなかった yuumei dewa nakatta ->

-> was not famous

Formal

To convey formality, na-adjectives used as a verb will take the following forms:

Present -> 有名です yuumei desu

Present Negative -> 有名ではありません yuumei dewa arimasen

Past -> 有名でした yuumei deshita

Past Negative -> 有名ではありませんでした yuumei dewa arimasen deshita

List of i-Adjectives

Hiragana	Kanji	Romaji	English
あぶない	危ない	abunai	dangerous
あかい	赤い	akai	red
あかるい	明るい	akarui	bright, light
あまい	甘い	amai	sweet
あおい	青い	aoi	blue
あたらしい	新しい	atarashii	new
あたたかい	温かい	atatakai	warm
あつい	暑い	atsui	hot (air)
あつい	厚い	atsui	thick
ちいさい	小さい	chiisai	small
ちかい	近い	chikai	near, close
ふるい	古い	furui	old
ふとい	太い	futoi	fat, thick
はやい	早い	hayai	early
はやい	速い	hayai	quick, fast
ひくい	低い	hikui	low
ひろい	広い	hiroi	spacious,wide
ほしい	欲しい	hoshii	to want something
ほそい	細い	hosoi	fine, thin
いそがしい	忙しい	isogashii	busy
いたい	痛い	itai	painful
からい	辛い	karai	hot, spicy
かるい	軽い	karui	light (not heavy)
かわいい	可愛い	kawaii	cute, pretty
きいろい	黄色い	kiiroi	yellow
きたない	汚い	kitanai	dirty
くらい	暗い	kurai	dark
くろい	黒い	kuroi	black

まるい	丸い	marui	round
まずい	不味い	mazui	bad tasting
みじかい	短い	mijikai	short
むずかしい	難しい	muzukashii	difficult
ながい	長い	nagai	long
おいしい	美味しい	oishii	delicious, tasty
おもい	重い	omoi	heavy
おもしろい	面白い	omoshiroi	intersting, funny
おおきい	大きい	ookii	big
おそい	遅い	osoi	late, slow
さむい	寒い	samui	cold
せまい	狭い	semai	narrow
しろい	白い	shiroi	white
すずしい	涼しい	suzushii	cool
たかい	高い	takai	expensive, high
たのしい	楽しい	tanoshii	pleasant, enjoyable
とおい	遠い	tooi	far
つまらない	詰らない	tsumaranai	uninteresting
つめたい	冷たい	tsumetai	cold
つよい	強い	tsuyoi	strong
うすい	薄い	usui	thin
わかい	若い	wakai	young
やさしい	優しい	yasashii	gentle
やすい	安い	yasui	cheap
よい / いい	良い	yoi / ii	good

List of na-adjectives

Hiragana	Kanji	Romaji	English
ひつよう	必要	hitsuyou	necessary
	いや	iya	unpleasant
じゆう	自由	jiyuu	free, unrestrained
じょうぶ	丈夫	joubu	healthy, robust
じょうず	上手	jyouzu	good, skilled
きけん	危険	kiken	dangerous
きれい	きれい	kirei	beautiful, pretty

らく	楽	raku	easy, comfortable
すき	好き	suki	love, like
たいへん	大変	taihen	terrible
ゆうめい	有名	yuumei	famous
ざんねん	残念	zannen	disappointing, regrettable
べんり	便利	benri	useful, convenient
だいじょうぶ	大丈夫	daijoubu	fine, okay
だいすき	大好き	daisuki	passionate
げんき	元気	genki	healthy
へた	下手	heta	bad at, unskilled
ひま	暇	hima	free (time)
いろいろ	色々	iroiro	various
いっしょうけんめい	一生懸命	isshoukenmei	to one's fullest possibility
じゅうぶん	十分	jyuubun	sufficient
けっこう	結構	Kekkou	enviable, wonderful
きらい	嫌い	kirai	to not like

	まじめ	majime	serious, earnest
まっすぐ	真直ぐ	massugu	straight
むり	無理	muri	unreasonnable
ねっしん	熱心	nesshin	eager, enthusiastic
にぎやか	賑やか	nigiyaka	lively
りっぱ	立派	rippa	splendid, fine, excellent
しんぱい	心配	shinpai	worry, care
しずか	静か	shizuka	quiet
たいせつ	大切	taisetsu	precious, important
ていねい	丁寧	teinei	polite
てきとう	適当	tekitou	suitable, proper
とくべつ	特別	tokubetsu	special

Chapter 9: Japanese Honorifics

When learning Japanese, you will have to familiarize yourself with "honorifics" to make sure that you're addressing people properly. Honorifics are suffixes that are commonly attached to people's names and titles when taking to or about them. They are the counterparts of English title prefixes such as Mister, Sir, Miss, Madam, and Dr.

Formal Honorifics

– sama

The honorific –sama is the most formal honorific suffix. It is used to refer to the royalty (ohimi-sama) and God (kami-sama).

-san

The honorific suffix –san is the most commonly used formal honorific. It approximates the titles Mr. and Ms. in English. In Japan, -san is used in pubic places and among colleagues and acquaintances. It is generally used in schools and offices among students and co-workeres.

Informal Honorifics

–chan

The suffix –chan is a familiar female honorific that implies endearment. It is commonly used to address children. It is also widely used among friends and family members. Women in the family generally use –chan to refer to one another. It can also be used for males.

-kun

The suffix –kun is the male counterpart of –chan. It is commonly used for children and among friends and peers. Within the family, -kun is generally not used to address grown or older men in the family.

-bō

The suffix –bō is reserved for little boys. This cutesy honorific was derived from obbochama which means "little lord". It is not appropriate to use it to address adult male.

Familial Honorifics

Japanese generally address older family members with honorifics. This is quite similar to how you would refer to older people with endearing titles like Dad, Mom, Grandpa, or Grandma.

Besides the formal title prefixes, elders can be addressed using acceptable informal title prefixes.

Here are the most commonly used and acceptable familial honorifics:

Root -> Formal -> Informal

Tō (father) -> Oto-san -> To-san

Kā (mother) -> Oka-san -> ka-san, ka-chan

Jī (grandfather) -> Ojī-san -> Ojī-chan

Bā (grandmother) -> Obā-san -> Obā-chan

Ba (aunt) -> Oba-san

Ji (uncle) -> Oji-san

Nii (older brother) -> Onii-san, Nii-san -> Onii-chan, Nii-chan, nii-san

Nē (older sister) -> Onē-san, Nē-san -> Onē-chan, Nē-chan, ne-san

Chapter 10: Asking Questions

When you want more information than yes-no response, you'll have to learn how to use Japanese interrogative words.

Asking Who

Using だれ　dare

The basic question word for who is だれ　dare. It is an informal question word that can only be used among family and friends.

You can place the question word before the verb and add か ka at the end.

For example:

あの ひとはだれですか。 -> Who is that person?

ano hito wa dare desu ka?

The response can be as simple as the name of the person with the verb です desu:

ジョンさんです

Jon-san desu

He is Mr. John.

It can also be stated in a full sentence such as:

あの ひとはジョンです。

Ano hito wa Jon-san desu.

That person is Mr. John.

Using どなた donata

When you want to show respect to the person you are asking about, you will have to use どなた donata instead of だれ dare. You will also need to use かた kata instead of ひと. The polite form is the preferred form when asking who questions. It is used to convey formality. If you're uncertain whether the situation is formal or informal, it is safe to use どなた donata.

Example:

あのかたはどなたですか。 -> Who is that person?

ano kata wa donata desuka?

Asking What is it

Using 何 Nan/Nani

The question word 何 nan/nani is used to ask "what" in Japanese. The nan form is used when asking "what' with desu while the nani form is used elsewhere.

Examples:

なんですか。 -> What is it?

Nan desu ka?

これはなんですか。 -> What is this?

Kore wa nan desu ka?

あの山は何ですか？ -> What is that mountain?

Ano yama wa nan desu ka?

To respond to nan/nani question, you can replace the question word with the identity of the item and drop the か ka question tag:

これはとけいです -> This is a watch.

Kore wa tokei desu

あの山はエベレストです -> That mountain is Mt. Everest

Ano yama wa eberesuto desu

When you use a question word as a subject, it has to be indicated as such by the particle が ga.

Example:

なにがおいしいですか。 -> What's delicious?

Nani ga oishī desu ka?

To respond, you can just replace the question word with the answer:

寿司がおいしいですか。 -> Sushi is delicious.

Sushi ga oishī desu

Asking Which

Using どれ dore and どの dono

The question word どれ dore is used to ask "which one". To ask which noun, you'll use the pattern どの dono + noun.

Example:

病院はどれですか。 -> Which is the hospital?

Byōin wa dore desu ka

病院はどの建物ですか。　-> Which building is the hospital?

Byōin wa dono tatemono desu ka

When asking which person and location, you'll use どの dono + noun.

Example:

アキさんはどの人ですか？ -> Which person is Mr. Aki?

Aki-san wa dono hito desu ka

Using どちら dochira to ask which

The question word どちら dochira is used in more formal situations.

The question word どちら dochira can be used to ask questions that compare two items. You will need to add the particle と (to) after each item then add どちらが (dochira ga) and the predicate in question format.

Example:

電車とバスとどちらが早いですか？ -> Which is faster, train or bus?

densha to basu to dochira ga hayai desu ka

Asking Where

The question word どこ doko is used to ask "where" something is in Japanese.

To ask where, simply place the object you're looking for before the topic marker は wa as shown in the following pattern:

＿＿＿ はどこですか。　-> ___ wa doko desu ka

Examples:

ホテルはどこですか？　-> Where is the hotel?

Hoteru wa doko desu ka?

どこ です か？　-> Where is it?

doko desu ka

In casual conversations, you can do away with 'desu ka' and simply say 'doko' to ask where.

Asking When

The question word いつ itsu is used to ask when.

Examples:

いつ 日本に きましたか? -> When did you come to Japan?

Itsu Nihon ni kimashita ka?

いついきますか？ -> When are you going?

itsu ikimasu ka?

いつ ですか？ -> When is it?

itsu desu ka

Asking Why

The question word どうして doushite is used to ask why in Japanese.

Examples:

どうして ですか？ -> Why?

doushite desu ka?

Acknowledging Information

When someone provides you with a response or information, it's common courtesy to acknowledge it. Here are some phrases that you can use:

ああ、そうですか -> Ā, sō desu ka -> Oh, is that so?/Oh, really?

そうですね。 -> sō desu ne -> So it is, isn't it?

そうですよ。 -> sō desu yo -> Yes, I agree.

Chapter 11: Expressing What You Want

Depending on the scenario, there are different ways to express what you want in Japanese.

The right word to use will vary depending on situations such as whether the object of desire is an object (noun) or an action (verb) or whether you're speaking to a peer or superior. The form will also differ whether you're asking a question or telling a statement.

Expressing a want involving a noun (object)

When the object of your desire is a noun like house, bag, or car, you will use "hoshii" which means "to want".

Examples:

私はバッグが欲しいです。

Watashi wa baggu ga hoshī desu.

I want a bag.

私はガールフレンドが欲しいです。

Watashi wa gārufurendo ga hoshī desu.

I want a girlfriend.

Expressing a want involving a verb (action)

If what you want is not an object but an action such as playing, drinking, or eating, it is expressed as "-tai desu".

Here's the basic sentence form to say what you want to do:

someone + wa + something + o –tai desu

Examples:

私はバッグを購入したいです。

Watashi wa baggu o kōnyū shitai desu.

I want to buy a bag.

私は朝食を食べたいです。

Watashi wa chōshoku o tabetai desu.

I want to eat breakfast.

If you want to place the emphasis on a subject, you will have to use the particle "ga" in place of the particle "o".

Example:

僕はケーキが食べたいです。

Boku wa kēki ga tabetai desu.

I want to eat cake.

Informal Situations

In familiar situations, you can drop 〜です desu.

Examples:

私はお金が欲しい。

Watashi wa okane ga hoshii.

I want money.

How to conjugate verbs to たい tai

The たい(tai) form is added after the verb ending to express that someone wants to perform an action.

Here's a quick guide on how to conjugate verbs to たい tai:

Group 1 Verbs

Group 1 verbs change their ending from –u to –I before adding たいtai.

Examples:

to read: -> 読む yomu > 読みたい yomitai

to buy: -> 買う kau > 買いたい kaitai

to go: -> 行く iku > 行きたい ikitai

to drink: -> 飲む nomu > 飲みたい nomitai

to hear/listen -> 聞く kiku > 聞きたい kikitai

Group 2 Verbs (-iru/-eru verbs)

Group 2 verbs drop the −ru ending and add たい at the end.

Examples:

to watch/see -> 見る miru > 見たい mitai

to wear -> 着る kiru > 着たい kitai

to eat -> 食べる taberu > 食べたい tabetai

to remember -> 覚える oboeru > 覚えたい oboetai

to leave/come out -> 出る deru > 出たい detai

Group 3 Verbs

The irregular verbs take the following −tai forms:

to come -> 来る kuru > 来たい kitai

to do -> する suru > したい shitai

When to use the −tai form

The −tai form is only used to express the desire of the first person and to ask that of the second person. It is not commonly used when asking for a superior's desire.

Examples:

私はヨーロッパに行きたいです。

Watashi wa yōroppa ni ikitai desu.

I want to go to Europe.

何が飲みたいですか?

Nani ga nomitai desu ka?

What do you want to drink?

Expressing that you don't want to do something

To say that you don't want to do something, you will have to add
たくない takunai instead of たい (tai):

Examples:

Group 1 Verbs

to buy -> 買う kau > 買いたくない kaitakunai

to go -> 行く iku > 行きたくない ikitakunai

Group 2 Verbs

to wear -> 着る kiru > 着たくない kitakunai

to watch/look -> 見る miru > 見たくない mitakunai

Group 3 Verbs

to do -> する suru > したくない shitakunai

to come -> 来る kuru > 来たくない kitakunai

Describing What a Third Person Wants

To talk about a third person's desire, you will use 欲しがっています "hoshigatte imasu" to express a desire for an object or the verb stem + 〜たがっています -tagatte imasu to express a desire for an action. Take note that the object of "hoshigatte imasu" is indicated by the particle を "o".

Examples:

私の妹はケーキを欲しがっています

Watashi no imōto wa kēki o hoshigatte imasu

My younger sister wants a cake.

ジョンはゲームを見たがっています。

Jon wa gēmu o mitagatte imasu.

John wants to watch the game.

健はカナダに行きたがっています。

Ken wa Kanada ni ikitagatte imasu.

Ken wants to go to Canada.

Expressing the Desire for Someone to Do Something for You

The "hoshii" expression is also used when you want someone to do something for you. The sentence pattern is "-te verb form hoshii". The particle "ni" is used to mark "someone".

Examples:

ジョンにたった今図書館に言って欲しいんです。

Jon ni tattaima toshokan ni itte hoshii n desu.

I want John to go to the library right now.

バッグを彼女に届けて欲しいですか。

Baggu o kanojo ni todokete hoshii desu ka

Do you want me to deliver the bag to her?

You can also express the same idea using "-te moraitai".

Examples:

私はジョンに運転してもらいたい。

Watashi wa Jon ni unten shite moraitai desu.

I want John to drive.

私はあなたに本を読んでもらいたい。

Watashi wa anata ni hon o yonde moraitai desu.

I want you to read me a book.

You can use the same pattern to state a desire for a superior to do something. For this purpose, you can use the "itadaku", the humble counterpart of "morau".

Examples:

私はたかし先生に来ていただきたい。

Watashi wa Takashi-sensei ni kite itadakitai.

I would like Professor Takashi to come.

Chapter 12 Japanese Numbers and Counters

Cardinal Numbers

Japanese numbers, by themselves, are not that difficult to learn. Although there are some variations in pronunciation, counting is straightforward. You will have to memorize the numbers one to ten as these are unique numbers. You will be using them to form the succeeding numbers.

Here are the numbers one to ten:

	Romaji	Hiragana	Kanji
1	ichi	いち	一
2	ni	に	二
3	san	さん	三
4	shi/yon	し・よん	四
5	go	ご	五
6	roku	ろく	六
7	shichi/nana	しち・なな	七
8	hachi	はち	八
9	kyū/ku	きゅう・く	九
10	jū	じゅう	十

Take note that the numbers 4, 7, and 9 have two pronunciations. The first pronunciation is the on'yomi or Chinese pronunciation. For both numbers 4 and 7, the second pronunciation given was derived from Old Japanese. For number 9, 'ku' was derived from Chinese readings. You can use either pronunciation when reciting the numbers or counting. When you need to count something, however, you can only use one pronunciation in most cases as determined by the counter.

The numbers 11 to 19 are pronounced differently. The number 11, for instance, can be translated as "ten-one", number 12 as "ten-two", and so on up to number 19

	Romaji	Hiragana	Kanji
11	jū-ichi	じゅういち	十一
12	jū-ni	じゅうに	十二
13	jū-san	じゅうさん	十三
14	jū-shi/jū-yon	じゅうし・じゅうよん	十四
15	jū-go	じゅうご	十五
16	jū-roku	じゅうろく	十六
17	jū-shichi/jū-nana	じゅうしち・じゅうなな	十七
18	jū-hachi	じゅうはち	十八
19	jū-kyū	じゅうきゅう	十九

The number 20, にじゅう ni-jū, literally means two-ten. For the succeeding numbers up to 29, you will simply append the units like what you did for the numbers 11 to 19. Hence, number twenty-one is ni-jū-ichi (two-ten one), number twenty-two is ni-jū-ni (two-ten two), and so on up to the number 29.

	Romaji	Hiragana	Kanji
20	nijū	にじゅう	二十
21	nijū-ichi	にじゅういち	二十一
22	nijū-ni	にじゅうに	二十二
23	nijū-san	にじゅうさん	二十三
24	nijū-shi/nijū-yon	にじゅうし・にじゅうよん	二十四
25	nijū-go	にじゅうご	二十五
26	nijū-roku	にじゅうろく	二十六
27	nijū-shichi/nijū-nana	にじゅうしち・にじゅうなな	二十\七
28	nijū-hachi	にじゅうはち	二十八
29	nijū-kyū	にじゅうきゅう	二十九

For the other tens digits up to ninety, you'll follow the same rule and just add the units digits to the tens.

Here are the other tens digits:

	Romaji	Hiragana	Kanji
30	san-jû	さんじゅう	三十
40	yon-jû	よんじゅう	四十
50	go-jû	ごじゅう	五十
60	roku-jû	ろくじゅう	六十
70	nana-jû	ななじゅう	七十
80	hachi-jû	はちじゅう	八十
90	kyû-jû	きゅうじゅう	九十

Number 100, ひゃく hyaku, is another unique number that you should memorize.

	Romaji	Hiragana	Kanji
100	hyaku	ひゃく	百

To write 101, you just need to combine hyaku+ichi, hyaku-ichi ひゃくいち or literally, one hundred-one. You will do the same for the rest of the numbers 102 to 199.

	Romaji	Hiragana	Kanji
101	hyaku-ichi	ひゃくいち	百一
110	hyaku-ju	ひゃくじゅう	百十
150	hyaku go-ju	ひゃくごじゅう	百五十
160	hyaku roku-ju	ひゃくろくじゅう	百六十
170	hyaku nana-ju	ひゃくななじゅう	百七十
180	hyaku hachi-ju	ひゃくはちじゅう	百八十
190	hyaku kyu-ju	ひゃくきゅうじゅう	百九十
199	hyaku kyu-ju kyu	ひゃくきゅうじゅうきゅう	百九十九

108

The process is repeated when you reach 200 and so on up to 999. The number 1,000 is another distinct number that you should memorize. Applying the same strategy used to name smaller numbers, you'll simply write 1,000 and add the smaller number.

Here are the bigger Japanese numbers:

	Romaji	Hiragana	Kanji
200	nihyaku	にひゃく	二百
300	sanbyaku	さんびゃく	三百
400	yonhyaku	よんひゃく	四百
500	gohyaku	ごひゃく	五百
600	roppyaku	ろっびゃく	六百
700	nanahyaku	ななひゃく	七百
800	happyaku	はっぴゃく	八百
900	kyuuhyaku	きゅうひゃく	九百
1,000	sen	せん	千
2,000	nisen	にせん	二千
3,000	sanzen	さんぜん	三千
4,000	yonsen	よんせん	四千
5,000	gosen	ごせん	五千
6,000	rokusen	ろくせん	六千
7,000	nanasen	ななせん	七千
8,000	hassen	はっせん	八千
9,000	kyuusen	きゅうせん	九千
10,000	ichiman	まん	万
20,000	niman	にまん	二万
1,000,000	hyakuman	ひゃくまん	百万
2,000,000	nihyakuman	にひゃくまん	二百万
1,000,000,000	juoku	じゅうおく	十億

Counters

Now that you have familiarized yourself with Japanese numbers, you're ready to start learning how to count in Japanese. Japanese uses a variety of counters to count different types of objects. They are attached directly to a number to indicate the quantity of an object. A counter indicates what type of object is being counted. They are usually based on the object's shape or size.

For example, if you count an object like a shirt, you'll have to attach まい (mai), the counter for flat and thin objects. Hence, to count three shirts, you'll say:

シャツさんまい -> shatsu san-mai -> three shirts

To say three books, you'll use the counter さつ satsu:

ほんさんさつ -> hon san-satsu -> three books

Take note that some numbers change their pronunciation when attached to a certain counter. Hence, you will have to learn how each number is pronounced with each counter.

Here are the most frequently used counters:

Objects

Romaji	Kana	Kanji	Usage
dai	だい	台	machines, vehicles and similar objects
hai	はい	杯	liquid in containers such as glasses, cups, and bowls

hon	ほん	本	pens, trees, and other long and cylindrical objects
kai	かい	階	building floor
ken	けん	件	buildings, houses
ko	こ	個	compact and small objects
mai	まい	枚	paper, dishes, stamps, and other thin and flat objects
satsu	さつ	冊	books, magazines, photo album, and other bound objects
soku	そく	足	footwear pairs: shoes, socks, stockings, etc.
tsū	つう	通	letters

Duration

jikan	じかん	時間 -	hour
fun	ふん	分	minute
byō	びょう	秒	second
shū	しゅう	週	week

kagetsu	かげつ	か月	month
nen	ねん	年	year, school year

Frequency

do	ど	度	number of times, occurrences
kai	かい	回	number of times, occurrences

Order

ban	ばん	番	ordinal numbers, position, form

People

nin	にん	人	person
mei	めい	名	person, more polite than "nin"

Animals

hiki	ひき	匹	cats, dogs, fish, insects, and other small animals
tō	とう	頭	bears, elephant,

			horses, and other large animals
wa	わ	羽	birds

Others

sai	さい	歳/才	age

The following tables will demonstrate how counting is done using the different counters:

satsu -> さつ -> Books, Magazines, and other bound objects

1	いっさつ	issatsu
2	にさつ	nisatsu
3	さんさつ	sansatsu
4	よんさつ	yonsatsu
5	ごさつ	gosatsu
6	ろくさつ	rokusatsu
7	ななさつ	nanasatsu
8	はっさつ	hassatsu
9	きゅうさつ	kyusatsu
10	じゅっさつ	jissatsu

The question word for "how many books" is なんさつ nansatsu.

本はなんさつありますか -> How many books are there?

Hon wa nansatsu arimasu ka

ほん がはっさつ あります -> There are eight books.

Hon ga hassatsu arimasu

hiki ひき -> cats, dogs, fish, insects, and other small animals

1	いっぴき	ippiki
2	にひき	nihiki
3	さんびき	sanbiki
4	よんひき	yonhiki
5	ごひき	gohiki
6	ろっぴき	roppiki
7	ななひき	nanahiki
8	はっぴき	happiki
9	きゅうひき	kyūhiki
10	じゅっぴき	juppiki

The question word to ask "how many small animals"

is -> なんびき-> nanbiki.

犬はなんびきいますか -> How many dogs are there?

Inu wa nanbiki imasu ka

犬がごひきいます -> There are five dogs.

Inu ga gohiki imasu

tou -> とう -> bears, elephant, horses, and other large animals

1	いっとう	ittou
2	にとう	nitou
3	さんとう	santou
4	よんとう	yontou
5	ごとう	gotou
6	ろくとう	rokutou
7	ななとう	nanatou
8	はっとう	hattou
9	きゅうとう	kyūtou
10	じゅっとう	juttou

The question word for "how many large animals"

is なんとう nantou.

ぞうはなんとういますか？ -> How many elephants are there?

Zō wa nantou imasu ka?

ぞうがよんとういます -> There are four elephants.

Zō ga yontou imasu

nin -> 人 -> person

1	ひとり	hitori
2	ふたり	futari
3	さんにん	sannin
4	よにん	yonin
5	ごにん	gonin
6	ろくにん	rokunin
7	しちにん	shichinin
8	はちにん	hachinin
9	きゅうにん	kyūnin
10	じゅうにん	jūnin

The question word for "how many persons" is　なんにん nannin.

むすこがさんにんいます。 -> I have three sons.

Musuko ga sannin imasu.

友達がふたり来ます。　-> Two friends are coming.

Tomodachi ga futari kimasu.

mai まい　　paper, dishes, stamps, and other thin and flat objects

1	いちまい	ichimai
2	にまい	nimai
3	さんまい	sanmai
4	よんまい	yonmai
5	ごまい	gomai
6	ろくまい	rokumai
7	ななまい	nanamai
8	はちまい	hachimai
9	きゅうまい	kyūmai
10	じゅうまい	jūmai

The question word for "how many flat object?" is -> なんまい -> nanmai.

お皿がにまいあります。　-> There are two plates.

Osara ga nimai arimasu

hon -> ほん -> pens, trees, and other long and cylindrical objects

1	いっぽん	ippon
2	にほん	nihon
3	さんぼん	sanbon
4	よんほん	yonhon
5	ごほん	gohon
6	ろっぽん	roppon
7	ななほん	nanahon
8	はっぽん	happon
9	きゅうほん	kyūhon
10	じゅっぽん	jupon

The question word for "how many' is -> なんほん -> nanbon.

ネクタイをごほん買いました。 -> I bought five neckties.

Nekutai o gohon kaimashita.

dai -> だい -> machines, vehicles and similar objects

1	いちだい	ichidai
2	にだい	nidai
3	さんだい	sandai

4	よんだい	yondai
5	ごだい	godai
6	ろくだい	rokudai
7	ななだい	nanadai
8	はちだい	hachidai
9	きゅうだい	kyūdai
10	じゅうだい	juudai

The question word for "how many vehicles/machines" is ->
なんだい -> nandai.

私のちちは車をさんだい持っています。 -> My father has three cars.

Watashi no chichi wa kuruma o sandai motteimasu.

Special Japanese Numbers

While counters are essential, there's another way of counting in Japanese that doesn't require a counter. This system of counting makes use of traditional numerals in Japanese. You may need to mention beforehand the name of the counter to avoid confusion. These numbers may also be used for generic objects.

Number	Romaji	Hiragana	Kanji
1	hitotsu	ひとつ	一つ
2	futatsu	ふたつ	二つ

3	mittsu	みっつ	三つ
4	yottsu	よっつ	四つ
5	itsutsu	いつつ	五つ
6	muttsu	むっつ	六つ
7	nanatsu	ななつ	七つ
8	yattsu	やっつ	八つ
9	kokonotsu	ここのつ	九つ
10	tō	とお	十
100	hyaku	ひゃく	百
1,000	sen	せん	千

Chapter 13 Months, Days, and Seasons

Months of the Year

The Kanji character 月 means month. The character before it denotes one to twelve to indicate the month of the year. Take note that the same Kanji characters are used to write the names of the month in both Japanese and Chinese but they differ in pronunciation. Arabic numbers may also be used before the 月 month character like 1月 to indicate January, 2月 February, and so on.

English	Kanji	Hiragana	Romaji
January	一月	いちがつ	ichigatsu
February	二月	にがつ	nigatsu
March	三月	さんがつ	sangatsu
April	四月	しがつ	shigatsu
May	五月	ごがつ	gogatsu
June	六月	ろくがつ	rokugatsu
July	七月	しちがつ	shichigatsu
August	八月	はちがつ	hachigatsu
September	九月	くがつ	kugatsu
October	十月	じゅうがつ	juugatsu
November	十一月	じゅういちがつ	juuichigatsu
December	十二月	じゅうにがつ	juunigatsu

Days of the Week

English	Kanji	Hiragana	Romaji
Sunday	日曜日	にちようび	nichiyōbi
Monday	月曜日	げつようび	getsuyōbi
Tuesday	火曜日	かようび	kayōbi
Wednesday	水曜日	すいようび	suiyōbi
Thursday	木曜日	もくようび	mokuyōbi
Friday	金曜日	きんようび	kinyōbi
Saturday	土曜日	どようび	doyōbi

The Kanji characters for each day of the week denote the following:

日 -> sun

月 -> moon

火 -> fire

水 -> water

木 -> wood

金 -> gold

土 -> earth

Days of the Month

Day	English	Hiragana	Romaji	Kanji
1	1st	ついたち	tsuitachi	一日
2	2nd	ふつか	futsuka	二日
3	3rd	みっか	mikka	三日
4	4th	よっか	yokka	四日
5	5th	いつか	itsuka	五日
6	6th	むいか	muika	六日
7	7th	なのか	nanoka	七日
8	8th	ようか	youka	八日
9	9th	ここのか	kokonoka	九日
10	10th	とおか	tōka	十日
11	11th	じゅういちにち	juuichinichi	十一日
12	12th	じゅうににち	juuninichi	十二日
13	13th	じゅうさんにち	juusannichi	十三日
14	14th	じゅうよんにち	juuyonnichi	十四日
15	15th	じゅうごにち	juugonichi	十五日
16	16th	じゅうろくにち	juurokunichi	十六日
17	17th	じゅうしちにち	juushichinichi	十七日
18	18th	じゅうはちにち	juuhachinichi	十八日
19	19th	じゅうくにち	juukunichi	十九日
20	20th	はつか	hatsuka	二十日

21	21st	にじゅういちにち	nijuuichinichi	二十一日
22	22nd	にじゅうににち	nijuuninichi	二十二日
23	23rd	にじゅうさんにち	nijuusannichi	二十三日
24	24th	にじゅうよんにち	nijuuyonnichi	二十四日
25	25th	にじゅうごにち	nijuugonichi	二十五日
26	26th	にじゅうろくにち	nijuurokunichi	二十六日
27	27th	にじゅうしちにち	nijuushichinichi	二十七日
28	28th	にじゅうはちにち	nijuuhachinichi	二十八日
29	29th	にじゅうくにち	nijuukunichi	二十九日
30	30th	さんじゅうにち	sanjuunichi	三十日
31	31st	さんじゅういちにち	sanjuuichinichi	三十一日

Seasons of the Year

English	Hiragana	Romaji	Kanji
season	きせつ	kisetsu	季節
winter	ふゆ	fuyu	冬
spring	はる	haru	春
summer	なつ	natsu	夏
fall/autumn	あき	aki	秋

Chapter 14: Telling Time and Date

Knowing how to tell time and date are important language skills that you will use on a daily basis.

Telling Time

If you want to find out what time is it, you will use the following phrase:

いま、なんじですか？ -> What time is it now?

Ima, nan-ji desu ka?

Here's a simpler way of asking for time:

なんじですか？ -> What time is it?

Nan-ji desu ka

To tell time, you have to familiarize yourself with Japanese numbers.

Expressing Time in Hours

The hours of the day are indicated by the suffix 〜時 ji which means "hour". The time in hours is often written in either Kanji or Arabic numerals. It is also quite common to see them in digital format such as 12:00 or 1:00.

To express the exact time in hours, you can use the following table:

English	Arabic	Kanji	Hiragana	Romaji
1 o'clock	1 時	一時	いちじ	ichi-ji
2 o'clock	2 時	二時	にじ	ni-ji
3 o'clock	3 時	三時	さんじ	san-ji
4 o'clock	4 時	四時	よじ	yo-ji
5 o'clock	5 時	五時	ごじ	go-ji
6 o'clock	6 時	六時	ろくじ	roku-ji
7 o'clock	7 時	七時	しちじ	shichi-ji
8 o'clock	8 時	八時	はちじ	hachi-ji
9 o'clock	9 時	九時	くじ	ku-ji
10 o'clock	1 0 時	十時	じゅうじ	juu-ji

11 o'clock	1 1 時	十一時	じゅういちじ	juuichi-ji
12 o'clock	1 2 時	十二時	じゅうにじ	juuni-ji

Take note of the three exceptions in pronunciation when stating the hour of the day:

4 o'clock -> yo-ji, not yon-ji

7 o'clock -> shichi-ji, not nana-ji

9 o'clock -> ku-ji, not kyuu-ji

To tell the exact time in hours, just add 'desu' after the time:

いちじです -> ichi-ji desu -> It's 1 o'clock.

くじです -> ku-ji desu -> It's 9 o'clock.

To express half hour after the hour, you will use the suffix 半 (han) which means half.

Examples:

1:30 -> いちじ半 -> chi-ji han -> 1 時半

2:30 -> にじ半 -> ni-ji han -> 2 時半

3:30 -> さんじ半 -> san-ji han -> 3 時半

4:40 -> よじ半 -> yo-ji han -> 4 時半

5:30 -> ごじ半 -> go-ji han -> 5 時半

Expressing Time in Minutes

To express the minutes, you will have to be familiar with the numbers from 1 to 59. The minutes are indicated by the suffix ～分 which can be pronounced as fun or pun depending on the number. The suffix ～分 is the equivalent of "minutes" when you're telling time in English.

The following table will illustrate the use of fun and pun and the corresponding transformation to certain numbers:

Arabic	Kanji	Hiragana	romaji
5分	五分	ごふん	gofun
10分	十分	じゅっぷん	juppun

When ご (go) and ふん(fun) was combined to express five minutes, there was no change in pronunciation. However, in the second example, you'll have to combine juu and fun to express then minutes. The resulting pronunciation of juppun was derived by implementing the following changes:

128

juu > jup + fun > pun = juppun

The same rule is used for bigger numbers:

Arabic	Kanji	Hiragana	romaji
１５分	十五分	じゅうごふん	juugofun
２０分	二十分	にじゅっぷん	nijuppun
５５分	五十五分	ごじゅうごふん	gojuugofun

The following table shows the changes for other numbers:

Arabic	Kanji	Hiragana	romaji
１分	一分	いっぷん	ippun
２分	二分	にふん	nifun
３分	三分	さんぷん	sanpun
４分	四分	よんぷん	yonpun
５分	五分	ごふん	gofun
６分	六分	ろっぷん	roppun
７分	七分	ななふん	nanafun
８分	八分	はっぷん	happun
９分	九分	きゅうふん	kyuufun
１０分	十分	じゅっぷん	juppun

When telling time with minutes, the minutes are expressed after the hour.

Examples:

It's 7:50 -> 7時10分 -> しちじじゅっぷんです shichiji juppun desu

It's 435 -> 4時35分 -> よじさんじゅうごふんです yoji sanjūgofun desu

It's 9:50 -> 9時50分 -> くじ五十分です kuji gojuppun desu

Useful Time Expressions

ごぜん -> gozen -> before noon AM

ごご -> gogo -> after noon PM

時間 -> jikan -> time

前 -> mae -> before

時計 -> tokei -> clock

朝 -> asa -> morning

夜 -> yoru -> night

晩 -> ban -> evening

昼 -> hiru -> noon

Telling the Date

To ask somebody for the date today, you can say:

今日は何日ですか。 -> What's the date today?

Kyō wa nan niche desu ka.

To express the complete date in Japanese, you have to provide the information in the following order: year, month, day of the month, and day of the week. The suffix −nen is added right afer the figure for the year.

To say, for example, that today is October 6, 2017, Friday, here's how the date is typically expressed:

今日は2017年10月6日金曜日です

Here's the breakdown of the date:

今日は kyô wa -> today

2017年 ni-sen jū nana-sen -> year 2017

10月 jū-gatsu -> October

6日 muika -> 6th day

金曜日 kinyōbi -> Friday

です desu -> to be

Here are other date examples:

8月１６日 -> hachi-gatsu jūroku-nichi -> August 16

１５日です。 -> jūgonichi desu -> It's the 15th of the month.

Useful Phrases

今日	kyō	today
本日	honjitsu	today (formal)
明日	ashita	tomorrow
あさって	asatte	the day after tomorrow
明日	asu	tomorrow (formal)
明後日	myōgonichi	the day after tomorrow
昨日	kinō	yesterday
(昨日	sakujitsu	yesterday (formal)
おととい	ototoi	the day before yesterday
来月	raigetsu	next month
今月	kongetsu	this month

先月	sengetsu	last month
再来月	saraigetsu	the month after next
先々月	sensengetsu	the month before last
毎年	maitoshi	every year
毎月	maitsuki	every month
毎週	maishū	every week
毎日	mainichi	every day
今年	kotoshi	this year
本年	honnen	this year (formal)

Chapter 15: Colors

The Japanese word for color is 色 iro. Color names can be used as a noun and adjective. Except for the primary colors, most color names are no-adjectives or noun forms. The no-adjectives are actually true nouns that take の (no) when used to modify nouns and the copular "desu" when used as a sentence predicate.

Primary Colors

All primary colors are i-adjectives:

red	あかい	akai
blue	あおい	aoi
yellow	きいろい	kiiroi
white	しろい	shiroi
black	くろい	kuroi

As with other i-adjectives, the color name is placed before the noun being described.

Examples:

きいろい とり -> a yellow bird

kiiroi tori

黒いふく -> black clothes

kuroi fuku

しろいマグ -> a white mug

shiroi magu

赤いはな

akai hana -> a red flower

あおいくるま -> a blue car

aoi kuruma

If you want to express, however, that something is of a particular color, you'll have to use the no-adjective or noun form of the color word. In such cases, the adjective is functioning as sentence predicate.

Here are the no-adjective forms of the primary colors:

English	Hiragana	Romaji
red	あか	aka
blue/green	あお	ao
yellow	きいろ	kiiro
white	しろ	shiro
black	くろ	kuro

Hence, while you will usually say あおいくるま aoi kuruma to refer to a blue car, the color blue will have to take on a different form when it is used as a predicate as shown in the following example:

くるまはあおです。 -> The car is blue. -> Kuruma wa ao desu

When referring to the color itself such as the "color yellow", you will use its noun form.

The noun forms are likewise used to form compound words like the following:

くろねこ -> kuroneko -> black cat

あかワイン -> akawain -> red wine

Other Color Names

The rest of the color names are nouns or no-adjectives:

light blue	みずいろ	mizuiro
dark blue	こん	kon
green	みどり	midori
orange	オレンジ	orenji
orange	オレンジいろ	orenjiiro
dark orange	だいだいいろ	daidaiiro
pink	ピンク	pinku
brown	ちゃいろ	chairo
violet/purple	むらさき	murasaki
grey	はいいろ	haiiro
lilac	ライラック	rairakku
silver	ぎんいろ	gin'iro
gold	きんいろ	kin'iro
bronze	せいどういろ	seidou iro
copper	あかがねいろ	akaganeiro
yellow green	きみどり	ki midori
beige	ベージュ	be-ju

As the above color names are nouns, you will have to add the particleの (no) when you want to use them as modifiers and the copula です(desu) when you want to use them as sentence predicate.

Examples:

みどりのかばんがほしい。 -> I want a green bag.

Midori no kaban ga hoshī.

かえるはみどりです。 -> Frogs are green.

Kaeru wa midori desu.

Take note that the colors blue and green are sometimes used interchangeably in Japan. Hence, a Japanese speaker may refer to the "green" traffic light as "blue".

The Japanese translation for "black and white" is 白黒 shiro kuro which means "white and black".

Asking what color is something

The question word なにいろ nani-iro is generally used to ask somebody "what color' something is.

なにいろですか。 -> What color is it?

Nani-iro desu ka?

みどりです。 -> It's green.

midori desu

No-adjectives

light blue	みずいろ	mizuiro
dark blue	こん	kon
green	みどり	midori
orange	オレンジ	orenji
orange	オレンジいろ	orenjiiro
dark orange	だいだいいろ	daidaiiro
pink	ピンク	pinku
brown	ちゃいろ	chairo
violet/purple	むらさき	murasaki
grey	はいいろ	haiiro
lilac	ライラック	rairakku
silver	ぎんいろ	gin'iro
gold	きんいろ	kin'iro
bronze	せいどういろ	seidou iro
copper	あかがねいろ	akaganeiro
yellow green	きみどり	ki midori
beige	ベージュ	be-ju

Chapter 16: Talking about Yourself and Your Family

Introducing Yourself

To introduce yourself in Japanese, you will typically start with the expression はじめまして (hajimemashite) which literally translates to "It's the first time (to meet you). This is equivalent to the English expression "Nice to meet you."

There are different ways to introduce yourself in Japanese.

A simple way is to state your name followed by the copula です(desu)

私は (name) です -> I'm (name).

Watashi wa (name) desu

Example:

私はマイケルです

Watashi wa Maikeru desu. -> I'm Michael.

You can also drop "watashi wa":

マイケルです -> I'm Michael.

Maikeru desu

Here's another way to introduce yourself:

私の名前は(name)です。 -> My name is ____.

Watashi no namae wa (name) desu

Example:

私の名前はマイケルです -> My name is Michael.

Watashi no namae wa Maikeru desu

After introducing yourself, you're expected to use a customary expression that Japanese people typically use during introductions:

よろしくお願いします。 -> Yoroshiku onegaishimasu

This is usually translated as "Please be nice to me" or "Please treat me well."

During introductions, you can exchange pleasantries and tell something more about yourself. Here are some common phrases:

こんにちは。初めまして。 -> Hello. Nice to meet you.

konnichiwa. Hajimemashite

To tell your nationality, you can say:

アメリカ人です。 -> I'm an American.

Amerikajin desu

To express your place of origin:

(Place) からきました kara kimashita

アメリカからきました -> I came from the United States.

Amerika kara kimashita

To state your age:

(age)歳です sai desu

１５さいです。 -> I'm fifteen years old.

jūgo sai desu

私は24歳です -> I'm 24 years old

Watashi wa 24-saidesu

To ask about someone's birthday and to state your birthday:

Here is a casual way to ask:

あなたの誕生日はいつですか。 -> When is your birthday?

anata no tanjōbi wa itsu desu ka

If you want to be more polite, you can ask:

お誕生日はいつですか。

o tanjōbi wa itsu desu ka?

To reply, you can say:

私の誕生日は (month) の (day)。

watashi no tanjōbi wa (month) no (day).

If your birthday is on June 10, you can state your birthday with:

私の誕生日はろくがつのとおか -> My birthday is on June 10th.

Watashi no tanjōbi wa rokugatsu no tōka.

To state your occupation:

(position)です desu

学生です。gakusei desu -> I'm a student.

私は弁護士です。 -> I'm a lawyer.

Watashi wa bengoshi desu.

私の仕事は(job) です。 -> My job is _____.

watashi no shigoto wa (job) desu.

私の仕事は経理です -> My job is accounting.

Watashi no shigoto wa keiri desu

Talking about Your Family

When talking about members of the family, be aware that there are different terms for each member depending on whose family you're talking about.

The familiar Japanese term for family is 家族 (kazoku). The formal term is ご家族 (gokazoku).

Japanese terms for family members vary depending on whether you're describing your own family to another person or when you're talking about the family of the other person.

When describing your own family, you will use the following terms for each member:

Kana	Kanji	Romaji	English
かぞく	家族	kazoku	Family/Family Members
そふ	祖父	sofu	Grandfather
そぼ	祖母	sobo	Grandmother
おじ	伯父	oji	Uncle (older than parent)
おじ	叔父	oji	Uncle (younger than parent)
おば	伯母	oba	Aunt (older than parent)
おば	叔母	oba	Aunt (younger than parent)
ちち	父	chichi	Father
はは	母	haha	Mother
りょうしん	両親	ryoushin	Parents
きょうだい	兄弟	kyoudai	Siblings/Brothers
しまい	姉妹	shimai	Sisters
あに	兄	ani	Older Brother
あね	姉	ane	Older Sister
おとうと	弟	otouto	Younger Brother
いもうと	妹	imouto	Younger Sister
ふうふ	夫婦	fuufu	Husband and Wife/Married

			Couple
しゅじん	主人	shujin	Husband
おっと	夫	otto	Husband
かない	家内	kanai	Wife
つま	妻	tsuma	Wife
いとこ	従兄弟	itoko	Male Cousin
いとこ	従姉妹	itoko	Female Cousin
こども	子供	kodomo	Children
むすこ	息子	musuko	Son
むすめ	娘	musume	Daughter
おい	甥	oi	Nephew
めい	姪	mei	Niece
まご	孫	mago	Grandchild
ぎりのあに	義理の兄	giri no ani	Brother-in-law (older than you)
ぎりのおとうと	義理の弟	giri no otouto	Brother-in-law (younger than you)
ぎりのむすこ	義理の息子	giri no musuko	Son-in-law
ぎりの〜	義理の〜	giri no ~	~-in-law

When talking about other people's family members, you will use the following terms to refer to each individual:

146

Kana	Kanji	Romaji	Meaning
ごかぞく	ご家族	go kazoku	Someone's Family/Family Members
おじいさん	お爺さん	ojii san	Grandfather
おばあさん	お婆さん	obaa san	Grandmother
おじさん	伯父さん	oji san	Uncle (Older than Parent)
おじさん	叔父さん	oji san	Uncle (Younger than Parent)
おばさん	伯母さん	oba san	Aunt (Older than Parent)
おばさん	叔母さん	oba san	Aunt (Younger than Parent)
ごりょうしん	ご両親	go ryoushin	Parents
おとうさん	お父さん	otou san	Father
おかあさん	お母さん	okaa san	Mother
ごきょうだい	ご兄弟	go kyoudai	Siblings
おにいさん	お兄さん	onii san	Older Brother
おねえさん	お姉さん	onee san	Older Sister
おとうとさん	弟さん	otouto san	Younger Brother
いもうとさん	妹さん	imouto san	Younger Sister
ごふうふ	ご夫婦	go fuufu	Husband and Wife/Married

			Couple
ごしゅじん	ご主人	go shujin	Husband
おくさん	奥さん	okusan	Wife
おこさん	お子さん	oko san	Children
むすこさん	息子さん	musuko san	Son
おじょうさん	お嬢さん	ojou san	Daughter
おまごさん	お孫さん	omago san	Grandchild

Here are common phrases you can use to describe yourself and your family:

To ask about the marital status of the other person:

結婚していますか。 Kekkon shiteimasu ka. -> Are you married?

The reply can be:

独身です。 -> Dokushin desu -> I am single.

結婚しています。 -> Kekkon shiteimasu -> I am married.

To ask about the number of children the other person has, you can say:

子供がいますか。　-> Kodomo ga imasu ka -> Do you have children?

The reply can be:

子供がひとりいます。　-> I have one child.

kodomo ga hitori imasu

子供がさんにんいます。　-> I have three children

kodomo ga sannin imasu

わたしは娘がいます。　-> I have a daughter.

watashi wa musume ga imasu

兄弟がいますか。　-> Do you have brothers and sisters?

Kyoudai ga imasu ka.

あにがふたりいます。　-> I have two older brothers.

Ani ga futari imasu

いもうとがひとりいます。 -> I have one younger sister.

Imouto ga hitori imasu.

私のおとうとは二十五歳です。 -> My younger brother is 25 years old.

Watashi no otōto wa nijūgosai desu.

私のおとうとはエンジニアです。 -> My younger brother is an engineer.

Watashi no otōto wa enjiniadesu.

私の母は親切です。 -> My mother is kind.

Watashi no haha wa shinsetsu desu.

Chapter 17: Useful Phrases

Greetings 挨拶 (aisatsu)

Greetings	Kana	Romaji
Good morning.	おはようございます	Ohayou gozaimasu
Good morning.	おはよう	Ohayou
Good afternoon.	こんにちは	Konnichiwa
Good evening.	こんばんは	Konbanwa
Goodnight.	おやすみなさい	Oyasuminasai
Goodbye.	さようなら	Sayounara
Thank you.	ありがとう	Arigatou
Thank you.	ありがとうございます	Arigatou gozaimasu
I'm sorry./Excuse me.	すみません	Sumimasen
No./Not at all.	いいえ	Iie
I'll go and come back.	いってきます	Ittekimasu
Please go and come back.	いってらしゃい	Itterashai
Welcome home.	おかえりなさい	Okaerinasai
I'm home.	ただいま	Tadaima

Thank you for the meal.	いただきます	Itadakimasu
Thank you for the meal.	ごちそうさま	Gochisousama
Nice to meet you.	はじめまして	Hajimemashite
Congratulations	おめでとうございます。	Omedetou gozaimasu.

Occupations

English	Kana	Rojami
Occupation	しょくぎょう	shoku gyou
Lawyer	べんごし	bengo shi
Hairdresser	びようし	biyou shi
Pastor/Clergyman	ぼくし	boku shi
Cook/Chef	ちょうりし	chouri shi
Carpenter	だいく	daiku
Engineer	エンジニア	enjinia
Producer/Director	えんしゅつか	enshutsu ka
Performing Musician	えんそうか	ensou ka
Speaker/Orator	えんぜつか	enzetsu ka
Real Estate Agent	ふどうさんぎょうしゃ	fudousan gyousha

152

Part-time Worker	フリーター	furi-ta-
Painter/Artist	がか	gaka
Artist	げいじゅつか	geijutsu ka
Engineer/Technologist	ぎし	gi shi
Bank Employee	ぎんこういん	ginkou in
Actor/Performer	はいゆう	haiyuu
Temporary Worker	はけんしゃいん	hakensha in
Soldier	へいし	hei shi
Secretary	ひしょ	hisho
Doctor	いしゃ	isha
Journalist	ジャーナリスト	ja-narisuto
Actress	じょゆう	joyuu
Scientist	かがくしゃ	kagaku sha
Accountant	かいけいし	kaikei shi
Company Employee	かいしゃいん	kaisha in
Female Nurse	かんごふ	kango fu
Nurse	かんごし	kango shi
Movie Director	かんとく	kantoku
Sport's Coach	かんとく	kantoku
Supervisor / Superintendent	かんとく	kantoku

Death from Overwork	かろうし	karoushi
Singer	かしゅ	kashu
Policeman	けいかん	kei kan
Security Guard	けいびいん	keibi in
Policeman	けいさつかん	keisatsu kan
Architect	けんちくか	kenchiku ka
Researcher	けんきゅういん	kenkyuu in
Pilot / Plane Captain	きちょう	kichou
Reporter	きしゃ	kisha
Cook	コック	kokku
Lecturer	こうし	kou shi
Government Worker	こうむいん	koumu in
Professor	きょうじゅ	kyouju
Teacher	きょうし	kyoushi
Unemployed Person	むしょくしゃ	mushoku sha
Farmer	のうみん	noumin
Office Lady/Female Office Worker	オーエル	o- eru
Policeman (Friendly term)	おまわりさん	omawari san
Pilot	パイロット	pairotto

Barber	りはつし	rihatsu shi
Fisherman	りょうし	ryou shi
Hunter	りょうし	ryou shi
Head Chef/Master Chef	りょうりちょう	ryouri chou
Cook/Chef	りょうりにん	ryouri nin
Judge	さいばんかん	saiban kan
Author/Writer	さっか	sakka
Soccer Player	サッカーせんしゅ	sakka-senshu
Salaried Employee	サラリーマン	sarari-man
Politician	せいじか	seiji ka
Teacher	せんせい	sensei
Photographer	しゃしんか	shashin ka
Chef	シェフ	shefu
Dentist	しかい	shikai
Firefighter/Fireman	しょうぼうし	shoubou shi
Stewardess	スチュワーデス	suchuwa-desu
Detective	たんてい	tantei
Shop Assistant	てんいん	ten in

Barber	とこや	tokoya
Driver/Chauffeur	うんてんしゅ	unten shu
Fortune teller	うらないし	uranai shi
Actor/Actress/Performer	やくしゃ	yakusha
Baseball Player	やきゅうせんしゅ	yakyuu senshu

Vegatables 野菜 yasai

English	Katakana	Romaji
asparagus	アスパラガス	asuparagasu
bamboo shoot	タケノコ	takenoko
bell pepper	ピーマン	piiman
broccoli	ブロッコリー	burokkorii
burdock	ゴボウ	gobou
cabbage	キャベツ	kyabetsu
carrot	ニンジン	ninjin
cauliflower	カリフラワー	karifurawaa
celery	セロリ	serori
Chinese cabbage	チンゲンサイ	chingensai
corn	トウモロコシ	toumorokoshi
cowpea	ササゲ	sasage

cucumber	キュウリ	kyuuri
eggplant	ナスビ/ナス	nasubi/nasu
garlic	ニンニク	ninniku
ginger	ショウガ	shouga
green soybeans	エダマメ	edamame
Japanese radish	ダイコン	daikon
Japanese mustard spinach	コマツナ	komatsuna
lettuce	レタス	retasu
lotus root	レンコン	renkon
mushroom	マッシュルーム	masshuruumu
mustard greens	カラシナ	karashina
onion	タマネギ	tamanegi
pea	エンドウ	endou
potato	ジャガイモ	jagaimo
pumpkin	カボチャ	kabocha
shiitake mushroom	シイタケ	shiitake
spinach	ホウレンソウ	hourensou
spring onion	ネギ	negi
sweet potato	サツマイモ	satsumaimo
taro	サトイモ	satoimo
tomato	トマト	tomato

water spinach	ヨウサイ	yousai
watercress	クレソン	kureson

Fruits くだもの kuda mono

English	Kana	Romaji
Fruit	くだもの	kuda mono
Fruit	フルーツ	furu-tsu
Apple	りんご / リンゴ	ringo
Apricot	あんず	anzu
Apricot	アプリコット	apurikotto
Avocado	アボカド	abokado
Banana	バナナ	banana
Blackberry	ブラックベリー	burakku beri-
Blueberry	ブルーベリー	buru- beri-
Cherry	サクランボ	sakuranbo
Cherry	チェリー	cheri-
Chestnut	クリ	kuri
Citron	ゆず	yuzu
Coconut	ココナッツ	kokonattsu
Durian	ドリアン	dorian
Fig	イチジク	ichijiku

Grape	ぶどう	budou
Grapefruit	グレープフルーツ	gure-pu furu-tsu
Guava	グアバ	guaba
Jackfruit	ジャックフルーツ	jakku furu-tsu
Kiwi	キウイ	kiui
Lemon	レモン	remon
Lime	ライム	raimu
Mandarin Orange	みかん	mikan
Mango	マンゴー	mango-
Melon	メロン	meron
Orange	オレンジ	orenji
Papaya	パパイヤ	papaiya
Peach	もも / モモ	momo
Pear	なし	nashi
Persimmon	カキ	kaki
Pineapple	パイナップル	painappuru
Plum	うめ	ume
Pomegranate	ざくろ	zakuro
Raisin	ほしぶどう	hoshi budou
Raspberry	きいちご	kiichigo

Raspberry	ラズベリー	razu beri-
Strawberry	いちご / イチゴ	ichigo
Watermelon	すいか / スイカ	suika

Clothes and Accessories

Clothes	いふく	ifuku
Clothing / Garment	いりょうひん	iryouhin
Belt	ベルト	beruto
Blazer	ブレザー	bureza-
Blouse	ブラウス	burausu
Boots	ブーツ	bu-tsu
Brassiere	ブラジャー	buraja-
Business Suit	せびろ	sebiro
Cardigan	カーディガン	ka-digan
Coat	コート	ko-to
Coat/Jacket	うわぎ	uwagi
Dress	ドレス	doresu
Earring	イヤリング	iyaringu
Hat/Cap	ぼうし	boushi
High Heeled Shoes	ハイヒール	haihi-ru
Jacket	ジャケット	jaketto
Japanese Summer	ゆかた	yukata

Kimono		
Jeans	ジーンズ	ji-nzu
Kimono	きもの	kimono
Necklace	ネックレス	nekkuresu
Necktie	ネクタイ	nekutai
Overcoat	オーバー	o-ba-
pajamas	パジャマ	pajama
Pierced Earring	ピアス	piasu
Raincoat	レインコート	reinko-to
Ring	ゆびわ	yubiwa
Sandals	サンダル	sandaru
Scarf	スカーフ	suka-fu
Shirt	シャツ	shatsu
Shoes	くつ	kutsu
Short Pants	はんズボン	hanzubon
Shorts	ショーツ	sho-tsu
Skirt	スカート	suka-to
Slacks	スラックス	surakkusu
Slippers	スリッパ	surippa
Sneakers	スニーカー	suni-ka-
Socks	くつした	kutsushita
Suit	スーツ	su-tsu

Sweat Shirt	トレーナー	tore-na-
Sweater	セーター	se-ta-
Swimwear / Swimsuit	みずぎ	mizugi
Trousers	ズボン	zubon
T-shirt	T-シャツ	T-shatsu
Underpants/Underwear	パンツ	pantsu
Underwear	したぎ	shitagi
White Shirt (Business Shirt)	ワイシャツ	waishatsu

Shopping Phrases

これはいくらですか。 Kore wa ikura desu ka.	How much is this?
見てもいいですか。 Mite mo ii desu ka.	Can I look at it?
要りません。 Irimasen	I don't want it.
はい、それにします。 Hai, sore ni shimasu	OK, I'll take it.
見ているだけです。	I'm just looking.

Miteiru dake desu.	
〜を探しています。ありますか？ ____ wo sagashi te imasu. Arimasu ka?	I'm looking for _____. Do you have them?

Restaurant Phrases

お飲み物は? onomi mono wa	Would you like a drink?
___を一つお願いします ___wo hitotsu onegai shimasu	Can I have one of _____?
お勧めは何ですか? osusume wa nan desu ka?	What do you recommend?
辛いですか？ Karai desu ka	Is it spicy?
甘いですか？ Amai desu ka	Is it sweet?
炒め物ですか？ Itamemono desu ka	Is it fried?
煮物ですか？	Is it cooked?

Nimono desu ka	
生ですか？ Nama desu ka	Is it raw?
お勘定をお願いします? okanjou wo onegai shimasu	Can I have the bill, please?
ごちそうさまでした gochisousama deshita	Thanks for the food.

Japanese Foods

English	Kana	Romaji
Food	たべもの	tabe mono
Japanese Food	にほんりょうり	nihon ryouri
breakfast	あさごはん	asa gohan
breakfast	ちょうしょく	chou shoku
lunch	ひるごはん	hiru gohan
lunch	ちゅうしょく	chuu shoku
dinner	ばんごはん	ban gohan
dinner	ゆうしょく	yuu shoku

supper	やしょく	ya shoku
side dish	おかず	okazu
snack/refreshment	おやつ	oyatsu
box lunch	べんとう	bentou
train station box lunch	えきべん	ekiben
meal/cooked rice	ごはん	gohan
seasonings/spices	ちょうみりょう	choumi ryou
bean curd/tofu	とうふ	toufu
beef	ぎゅうにく	gyuuniku
Buckwheat noodle	そば	soba
chicken meat	とりにく	toriniku
crab	かに	kani
cucumber	きゅうり	kyuuri
Curry and Rice	カレーライス	kare-raisu
Dumpling stuffed with minced pork	ギョウザ	gyouza
eel	うなぎ	unagi
egg	たまご	tamago
fish	さかな	sakana
Grilled chicken/broiled chicken	やきとり	yaki tori

Grilled meat cooked on iron plate	てっぱんやき	teppan yaki
Japanese bun filled with red bean paste	あんパン	anpan
Japanese horseradish	わさび	wasabi
Japanese style hotpot	しゃぶしゃぶ	shabu shabu
Lamb/mutton	ようにく	youniku
Miso soup	みそしる	miso shiru
Miso/bean paste	みそ	miso
Noodle made of wheat flour	うどん	udon
Octopus dumpling	たこやき	tako yaki
oil	あぶら	abura
onion	たまねぎ	tamanegi
pan fried noodle	やきそば	yaki soba
pepper	こしょう	koshou
pork	ぶたにく	butaniku
pork cutlet	とんカツ	tonkatsu
ramen	ラーメン	ra-men
Rice with beef and vegetable toppings	ぎゅうどん	gyuu don
Rice with boiled chicken and eggs	おやこどん	oyako

toppings		don
Rice with deep-fried prawns & fishes toppings	てんどん	ten don
Rice with glaze-grilled eel toppings	うなぎどん	unagi don
salt	しお	shio
shrimp/prawn	えび	ebi
sliced raw fish	さしみ	sashimi
soy sauce	しょうゆ	shouyu
steamed egg custard in tea cup	ちゃわんむし	chawan mushi
sticky rice cake	もち	mochi
sugar	さとう	satou
Sushi	すし	sushi
Tempura/deep-fried fish and vegetables	てんぷら	tenpura
Thin slices of beef cooked with vegetables	すきやき	suki yaki
vinegar	す	su
white bread/plain bread	しょくパン	shoku pan

Conclusion

I'd like to thank you and congratulate you for transiting my lines from start to finish.

I hope this book was able to help you to learn the fundamentals of the Japanese language quickly and easily.

Now is the time to practice your language skills, read Japanese short stories and newspapers, learn Kanji, and perhaps take a vacation to Japan.

I wish you the best of luck!

To your success,

Katasha Lee

Printed in the USA
CPSIA information can be obtained
at www.ICGtesting.com
LVHW050242151223
766590LV00033B/208